Also by Peter Baxter:
Rhodesia: Last Outpost of the British Empire
France in Centrafrique: From Bokassa and Operation Barracuda to the days of the EUFOR
Selous Scouts: Rhodesian Counter-Insurgency Specialists
SAAF's Border War: The South African Air Force in Combat, 1966–1989

Co-published in 2012 by:

Helion & Company Limited
26 Willow Road
Solihull
West Midlands
B91 1UE
England
Tel. 0121 705 3393
Fax 0121 711 4075
email: info@helion.co.uk
website: www.helion.co.uk

and

30° South Publishers (Pty) Ltd.
16 Ivy Road
Pinetown 3610
South Africa
email: info@30degreessouth.co.za
website: www.30degreessouth.co.za

Designed & typeset by Kerrin Cocks
Cover design by Kerrin Cocks
Printed in the UK by Henry Ling Limited, Dorchester, Dorset
and in South Africa by Pinetown Printers (Pty) Ltd, Pinetown, KwaZulu-Natal

ISBN 978-1-920143-70-1 (South Africa)
ISBN 978-1-908916-22-8 (UK)

British Library Cataloguing-in-Publication Data
A catalogue record for this book is available from the British Library

Cover photo: A British soldier captures a suspected Mau Mau insurgent.

Publisher's note
The publishers would like to apologise for the absence of the 8-page colour-plate section that ordinarily appears in the Africa@War series titles. The sourcing of colour photos has proved problematic in that, a) there is a severe paucity of colour photos from the Mau Mau era, and b) some owners have made the contribution of photographic material subject to their own personal political views.

CONTENTS

GLOSSARY and ABBREVIATIONS

Glossary

Baraza	a council of chiefs or elders
kipande	identification documents which all natives of the colony were required to carry
Kuke/Kukes	refers to Kikuyu
Micks/Mickeys	vernacular name applied by government forces to Mau Mau; Micky was short for Micky Mouse, implying the double initial M.
Muhimu	the Central Committee of Mau Mau responsible for organisation, logistics and political representation
Ngai	the supreme God in the religions of the Kamba, Kikuyu and Maasai nationalities of Kenya; according to the Kikuyu beliefs, he lives on the holy mountain *Kirinyaga*,or Mount Kenya.
Pax Britannia	those areas of the globe that came under British imperial protection; literally the *peace of Britain*.
posta	a location used as a 'post box' for internal Mau Mau communications and dispatches
simi	a panga, a machete-like utility knife in wide use throughout Africa
White Highlands	the Central Highlands, settled by whites

Abbreviations

EAA	East African Association
FIA	Field Intelligence Officer
GHQ	General Head Quarters
GOC	General Officer Commanding
HQ	Head Quarters
IBEAC	Imperial British East African Company
KAR	King's African Rifles
KA	Kikuyu Association
KCA	Kikuyu Central Association
KAU	Kenya African Union
PSYOPS	psychological operations
RAF	Royal Air Force
SITREP	situation report
SMLE	Short Magazine Lee Enfield

INTRODUCTION

"... a raw, ramshackle, crude and poverty stricken country with no tradition, history or pretence to civilisation and with only the railway as an excuse for its existence in the Empire"
—Elspeth Huxley, *White Man's Country*

There were two principal players in the drama of the Mau Mau uprising in Kenya: the Kikuyu, a federated Bantu-language group with deep ancestral ties to the region, and the more shallowly rooted white, English-speaking settler community of the late 19th and early 20th centuries. The core of the crisis lay in land, as it did in many similar episodes worldwide throughout the colonial period, and how the land was alienated and occupied by the incoming settler minority. There were, of course, many other side narratives that were also part of the cause and effect of violence in Kenya, but it was the land issue that generated the most acute cultural anxiety and anger among the Kikuyu people, who arguably suffered most, and indeed benefited most, out of all of Kenya's many ethnic groups from the brief period of European domination.

This fact is now broadly accepted by scholars and historians in the matter of what induced the Kikuyu to organise an armed rebellion, but at the time there was a great unwillingness on the part of the settler community, and to a large extent the wider British public, to acknowledge that a land crisis existed in the colony. It was this that fermented the tremendous hysteria that surrounded the episode, because, if no legitimate political or moral grievance could be identified, then what was taking place in the countryside could only be some sort of common derangement or savage reversion that was beyond the capacity of civilised man to comprehend. In fact, even the official term 'uprising' was arrived at with difficulty, with the Colonial Government of Kenya, and indeed the Imperial Government in London, both groping for some time to find a universally acceptable term to define precisely what was taking place in the colony. To have applied the term 'civil war', which in almost every respect this was, would have necessitated an open declaration of war, with all the political difficulties in a changing world that this would have implied. On the other hand, a simple 'civil disturbance', which this clearly was much more than, could, on paper at least, be dealt with by the civil authority, with military support made available only as and when it should be required. This, ultimately, was the pretence that was sustained, allowing the Mau Mau movement to be dealt with throughout its duration under a state of emergency, with all the amplified civil powers that could be squeezed from this.

A woman harvesting coffee in the early 1930s.

King's African Rifles.

There also was, and has since been, a war of propaganda waged between the British Government, as the ex-colonial power, and the Kenyan Government, and indeed many native Kenyans who fought or were active in one way or another during the period, as to who was the greater villain in a generally villainous episode, out of which, in truth, neither side has emerged with a great deal of credit.

There are, however, certain indisputable facts. Land alienation to whites in many areas of Africa took place towards the end of the 19th century, by which point an amalgamation of factors – cattle disease, famine and the depredations of the slave trade not least among them – had had the combined effect of reducing the native population of the land, which in turn created the fable that the land was unoccupied, and thus no one was significantly inconvenienced by the arrival and occupation of the land by the white man. Another inconvenient fact that is frequently ignored by blacks in their assessment of white merit during the period is that the arrival of large numbers of Europeans in east and southern Africa towards the end of the 19th century put an end to the slave trade, curbed the predations of one tribe against the other and introduced modern medicine and a predictability of food supply. This in turn resulted in an exploding native population and the consequent land hunger that followed. By then, of course, matters to a large extent had been established. The whites had settled the land, and, moreover, were making extremely productive use of it, while blacks found themselves in diminished native reserves which proved to be manifestly unequal to the demands of an exponentially growing population.

How did this process begin; what were the early signs? Jomo Kenyatta, the first independent leader of Kenya, and something of a founding father of the nation, had this comment attributed to him when pressed to answer this very question: "When the missionaries arrived, the Africans had the land and the missionaries had the Bible. They taught us how to pray with our eyes closed. When we opened them, they had the land and we had the Bible."[1]

And so to a large extent it was. Africa lay somnolent, undiscovered and undisturbed until Europe itself began to stir under the principals of enlightenment. The Age of Discovery saw the Portuguese probing southwards in search of a sea route to the Indies, which in turn opened up much of the coastal region of West Africa to an accelerated slave trade occasioned by the development of the settler economies of the Caribbean and the greater Americas. To ameliorate the tremendous suffering that this wrought upon the continent, a wave of Christian missionaries set forth who in due course permeated the interior and established protocols of interaction between their parent cultures and the significantly reduced, indeed almost skeletal remnants of black society. Those that had been plundered almost out of existence now grasped at any straw of salvation, even that requiring the primacy of an alien god whose alien priest promoted alien ritual.

Behind these came the explorers, and behind them the capitalists, until, last but by no means least, came the imperial governments who sectioned the continent according to their own metropolitan hierarchies and their own emerging Darwinian concepts of racial superiority.

The European mapping and exploration of East Africa began during the latter half of the 19th century, the most powerful impetus for which was the establishment of European consulates on the island of Zanzibar, which allowed for the formation of a safe base of operations from where expeditions of commercial and geographic exploration into the interior could be mounted.

Much of the early British interest in the region was stimulated by the abolition movement and a desire to drive the matter home on the ground. Later this motivation was usurped somewhat by commercial competition with the Germans, who, as latecomers to the African territorial bonanza, sought as wide an influence in East Africa as possible. Permanent British landfall was made in 1887 with the establishment of the Imperial British East African Company (IBEAC), and the lease from Seyyid Said, the Sultan of Muscat and Oman, whose seat of power was Zanzibar, of a

Jomo Kenyatta

A sign of the times.

ten-mile-wide strip of land on the coast. Chartered companies such as the IBEAC were at the time a very common instrument of imperial expansion across the European spectrum. The East India Company was perhaps the most famous of these, but the British South Africa Company and the Royal Niger Company where two such British companies that claimed and exploited significant swaths of territory in Africa. There was, in most cases, a philanthropic veneer to the actions and activities of these companies. This appealed very much to the Victorian self-image, and the general view that European empire offered an opportunity for salvation to the brutalised masses of Africa by the introduction of the twin tenets of legitimate commerce and Christian civilisation, which Cecil Rhodes, with characteristic pragmatism, described as "philanthropy plus five per cent".

The construction of the Uganda Railway defined Kenya as a British colony, or, perhaps more accurately, it defined East Africa from the port of Mombasa as far inland as modern-day Uganda as a British sphere of influence. The railway itself tended to have a greater symbolic and strategic than practical value in the first instance, with construction taking place at more or less the same time as a German financed railway line that was proceeding inland from the Indian Ocean port of Tanga to the Kilimanjaro region, with the two lines spaced little more than 60 miles apart from one another and following an almost identical trajectory.

The completion of the Uganda Railway as far as the eastern shore of Lake Victoria in 1901 opened up the territory, but to what end nobody quite knew. It could at least be said that a significant step had been taken towards the abolition of practical slavery thanks to the removal of the need for porter transit for all goods being traded in and out of the interior, but besides that, the £5 million price tag attached to the project hardly seemed justified by what East Africa had to offer. Eventually the IBEAC, accepting a financial liability of almost £200,000, ceded practical control of the entire enterprise of East Africa to the Crown. Thereafter, the question of what to do with this geographically splendid but economically insolvent territory became the responsibility of the first generation of colonial administrators. It was at this point, many have since concluded, that the serpent entered the Garden of Eden.

It was Sir Charles Eliot, the first British High Commissioner for East Africa, who is credited with the initial idea of introducing white agricultural settlement into the region as a means, in the first instance, of utilising the railway, and in the second of establishing a permanent white settler class in the colony.

Herewith, then, began the land saga.

At this point it becomes necessary to draw a distinction between how this overarching issue was viewed by those on either side of it, made somewhat easier by the fact that the division is clearly marked by race.

Historians of the period, almost all of whom were white, would not have it said that any hardship or dispossession was ever inflicted on blacks as a consequence of the white occupation of Kikuyuland, or what later became known as the White Highlands. This area is currently the Central Province of Kenya, and remains a temperate region situated adjacent to, and in between, the two highland massifs of the Aberdare Range and Mount Kenya. It lies largely above 5,000ft and was found at the period of occupation to be climatically suited to European settlement. Because at that time the landscape really was quite empty, it can with some fairness be said that the local black population was not initially inconvenienced by the arrival of the very few whites that settled there. In the words of Fred Majdalany, the first author and historian to attempt a chronicle of Mau Mau:

> It was only later, when the settler–African relationship was becoming a problem, that for political reasons the myth was created that the settlers had stolen their best land from the Africans because it was the most fertile. In fact it was not: only what they had done with it made it seem so and the only encroachment by the settlers was a small area of land in Kikuyu country near Nairobi ...[2]

However, everything, with a few exceptions, that was written at the time by whites has to be taken with a pinch of salt, quite as much as the highly embellished histories of the same period as written by many black academics in later years. The matter remains far too emotional for either party to reasonably write a balanced history, with current analysis by primarily British authors appearing to suffer an over-swing of the pendulum, with the condemnatory language of the 1950s and 1960s being replaced now by the deeply apologetic tones of a generation almost too indoctrinated by guilt.

Nonetheless, it is a little appreciated fact of the British Empire that ongoing friction existed between the Foreign and Colonial offices and local settler lobbies across Africa over the question of native land rights and labour. To the body politic of Whitehall the protection of native rights in British Africa was a matter of sacred trust, in particular in the aftermath of the First World War, and in fact an essential precondition for the leasing of any land to any European in Kenya was that it be proved to be unoccupied by any native.[3] This tenet was imposed by Whitehall on the settler community once it had begun to become clear that an ugly race dynamic was beginning to take form in the colony. Moreover, a fifth column of this emerging race conflict existed in the form of the East Indian, or Asian population as it was locally called, imported initially as labour for railway construction and later as imperial fighting men during the East Africa Campaign of the First World War. These, by the early 1920s, outnumbered whites significantly, and in keeping with the restive politics of the Indian mainland, had begun to demand greater political freedoms and representation. This prompted a speech to the House of Commons in 1923 by the then Colonial Secretary Victor Cavendish in the matter of resource dispensation in the East African colonies:

> Primarily Kenya is an African territory, and His Majesty's Government think it necessary definitely to record their considered opinion that the interests of the African natives must be paramount, and that if, and when, those interests and the interests of the immigrant races should conflict, the former should prevail. Obviously, the interests of the other communities, European, Indian or Arab, must severally be safeguarded ... But in the administration of Kenya His Majesty's Government regard themselves as exercising a trust on behalf of the African population, and they are unable to delegate or share this trust, the object of which may be defined as the protection and advancement of the native races.[4]

Whites at the time tended to regard African blacks in general as being steeply disadvantaged in the matter of development and progress, which is hard to argue against in the context of the times. They approached their relationship with local native communities with a high degree of paternalism and a sense that it was their moral duty as the civilising race to guide those in the kindergarten of life to full maturity under the sun with a stern yet fair hand. Many settlers in the midst of the crisis of the 1950s expressed genuine dismay and sadness that after all that they had done for their blacks they were being targeted and killed in such a grotesque manner. To many this was simply more evidence of a general lack of advanced capacity in blacks and even clearer reason why they needed to be handled firmly.

Despite this the aura of brutality and greed that came to exemplify the settler community as the drama of the Mau Mau unfolded was never entirely unjustified. The mild race-assimilationism that had characterised the period leading up to the Second World War evaporated soon afterwards, to be replaced by overt and growing racism generated by the clear threat to white interests occasioned by black nationalism and growing land hunger. There is nothing particularly unique about this, and it need not be seen in the context of race other than that race broadly defined the protagonists. In fact, it is the Kikuyu themselves in modern Kenya who are the target of more general accusations of a disproportionate amassing of wealth and power, and the corruption and violence necessary to achieve and maintain this has never been beyond their moral capacity.

However, the effect of white land alienation on the Kikuyu in particular has never been in doubt, and as populations began to rapidly increase under the *Pax Britannia* the seeds of inevitable conflict were sown. A trace of the bitterness felt generations after the fact is clearly discernible in the comments of Kenyan academic Wunyabari O. Maloba, who, in his excellent study of the episode, Mau Mau and Kenya: An Analysis of a Peasant Revolt, commented on the emotional debate that took place regarding the wisdom of settling Jews alongside white Christians on the Central Highlands: "At no time in these discussions," Maloba writes, "was any thought seriously entertained of using indigenous Africans as the agents of commercial agricultural production in Kenya. It was postulated that Africans were so primitive, so disorganised, that it would be centuries before they would be able to assume the gigantic task of commercial farming." The author went on to quote High Commissioner Charles Eliot himself on the matter:

> ... the African is greedy and covetous enough ... he is too indolent in his ways, and too disconnected in his ideas, to make any attempt to better himself, or to undertake any labour which does not produce a speedy visible result. His mind is far nearer to the animal world than that of the European or Asiatic, and exhibits something of the animals' placidity and want of desire to rise beyond the stage he has reached.[5]

This profoundly uncharitable comment was widely reflected in the attitudes of whites encountering for the first time the native African as he emerged from a generation or more of predation and difficulty, and was probably not without some justification in terms of how indigenous society might have appeared at the time. However, Eliot, as with many others, was not above constructing his theories to suit his long-term objectives. An interesting journal observation for the times, dated 1902, was that written by Colonel Richard Meinertzhagen, then a captain in the King's African Rifles, on the matter of a conversation with the High Commissioner over the question of how the future face of Kenya might look:

> He intends to confine the natives to reserves and use them as cheap labour. I suggested that the country belonged to the Africans; that their interests must prevail over the interests of strangers. He would not have it; he kept on using the word 'paramount' with reference to the claims of the Europeans. I said that someday the African would be educated and armed; that would lead to a clash.[6]

Meinertzhagen was an interesting character, and something of a rarity at the time inasmuch as he was a clear-thinking liberal who did not subscribe to the popular view that the black man lay centuries short of self-determination in a modern world, and could therefore comfortably be excluded from the process of mapping out a long-term future for the various settled colonies. His writings and memoirs are filled with similar observations and warnings regarding the inevitable evolution of black political aspiration in a contemporary context. He served during the First World War as an intelligence officer in support of British and Commonwealth forces as they pushed into the German-held Tanganyika territory, and his success in this role was probably due in large part to the fact that he had bothered to penetrate the deeper strata of black thinking and could recognise in broad tenets that it differed little from that of anyone else.

In the Kikuyu, however, Meinertzhagen appeared to recognise something unique. Of all the many tribal and language groups that make up the human quilt of Kenya, the Kikuyu seemed to him to be the most resourceful and energetic, and those most likely to be influenced, and indeed benefitted by the potential advantages of western civilisation. "I am sorry to leave the Kikuyu," he wrote in 1904, as he briefly left the colony for less interesting work in India, "... they are the most intelligent of the African tribes I have met: therefore they will be the most progressive under European guidance and will be more susceptible to subversive activities."[7]

And so it was. What the average white settler tended to see in the Kikuyu as simply an alertness to opportunity and a light-fingered cupidity, Meinertzhagen recognised as a people taking stock of the potentialities of a changing world. That they did in the end drift towards subversion, as he had predicted that they would, probably had less to do with any particular susceptibility to intrigue than a lack of practical alternatives. The Kikuyu as a group were both the architects and leaders of early black political development in Kenya, and so can probably, quite justifiably, be credited with above-average acumen and resourcefulness. This is hardly unique in human history, and that it ultimately led individuals within the political movement to as much misadventure as adventure is also hardly unique.

Of all this the average white settler in Kenya was ignorant. Most acquired whatever standard of Swahili was necessary to communicate with their workers, often of mixed tribal background, all of whom spoke Swahili for much the same reason, but made more practical use of their own individual dialects. Of these the vast majority of whites knew very little, and cared even less, leading to the consequence that all, even those Europeans in authority, were completely removed from the general black value system and thought process.

The land question was a perfect example of this. Yes, there had been no appreciable population of blacks in physical occupation of the land when it was alienated to whites, but just the simple introduction of individual land ownership in a legal sense had no meaning to most blacks. Even the subsequent landlessness that this eventually led to was not unprecedented in Kikuyu society, it was simply that within a cash economy, and a constitutionally governed state, the ramification on an individual of landlessness was now a great deal more severe.

In fairness, very few, if any, early whites had any access to the complexities of the Kikuyu system of land tenure, which were first made available in written form by Jomo Kenyatta in his anthropological discourse, *Facing Mount Kenya*. This impressive book articulates very clearly what many in the colony would rather have ignored. It also brought Kenyatta quite a lot of attention and personal acclaim from British metropolitan scholars and liberal politicians, which immediately created suspicion within Kenya that he had simply written the book to embellish his personal credentials in British academic and political circles.

Be that as it may, Kenyatta did make the very valid point that a detailed study on the part of the colonial authorities of general black land usage protocols would have been advisable before drawing up sweeping plans for white settlement. Kenyatta remarks:

> In studying the Gikuyu tribal organisation it is necessary to take into consideration land tenure as the most important factor in the social, political, religious and economic life of the tribe. As agriculturalists, the Gikuyu people depend entirely on the land. It supplies them with the material needs of life, through which spiritual and mental contentment is achieved. Communion with the ancestral spirits is perpetuated through contact with the soil in which the ancestors of the tribe lie buried. The Gikuyu consider the earth as the 'mother' of the tribe, for the reason that the mother bears her burden for about eight or nine moons while the child is in her womb.[8]

Needless to say the land alienation process went on, with the entrenchment of white land interests formalised by a series of ordinances which, in 1915, also formally established the Native Reserves. These reserves, as was similarly the case in Southern Rhodesia, were regarded initially as a stop-gap measure between the alienation of land to Europeans and the evolution of the black peasantry into a wage-earning agricultural and industrial proletariat.

Another pillar of colonial domination, one associated very much with the formation of the reserves and the greater organisation of tribal life, was the appointment of tribal chiefs for the purpose of expediting grassroots administration. These men were often not drawn from any tradition of local government and were answerable not to each other, or their constituency, but to the local District Commissioner. This was a policy pursued in other British African territories too, most notably the Rhodesias and Nyasaland, with a common theme emerging of widespread popular distrust towards the chiefs who were rightly recognised as being government appointees, wedded to official policy and the beneficiaries of much loyalty-dependent largesse.

Perhaps the last factor to come into play in the drama of Mau Mau was the combined effect of two World Wars, the Second World War perhaps being the most influential, on the direct growth of black militancy in the colony. The East Africa Campaign of the First World War pitted British and Commonwealth forces against a German colonial *Schutztruppe* under the command of the extremely highly regarded Colonel Paul Emile von Lettow-Vorbeck. Both sides made extensive use of native troops and ancillary personnel drawn from across German and British Africa. The East Africa Campaign of the Second World War, on the other hand, was fought mostly in the northern territories of Kenya and in Ethiopia and Somalia, but also using large numbers of native troops drawn from a variety of colonial battalions. Kenyan native manpower was used primarily within the King's African Rifles battalions, which saw action in both East Africa, the Horn of Africa and in South East Asia.

Large numbers of men thereafter returned home and were demobilised into society, bathed in the accolades of their imperial commanders and public at large, but with little practical effort or resource actually spared on their rehabilitation and reintroduction into society. One widely circulated comment made by a black solider of the times was that the white man came home from war and was given a farm; the black man came home and was given a bicycle. And this was quite true. Emigrating British ex-servicemen were indeed welcomed into the colony with generous grants of land and other incentives to settle, as they were elsewhere in British Africa. Nothing of the sort was offered to blacks.

Besides this, the worldwide social outlook in the post-war period tended to more nationalistic in flavour, corresponding to a general sense that the British Empire was entering its twilight, in particular with the epoch defining grant of independence to India achieved in 1947. Coupled with this, came the first generation of university- and higher-educated blacks in Africa who emerged into productive society with a far clearer understanding of European politics and a far greater capacity to embrace the demands of modern life than had been the lot of their parents.

In Kenya, political organisation began very early, and began largely, and unsurprisingly, as an innovation of the Kikuyu. In 1919, consequential to the mass demobilisation of native manpower from the colonial and support regiments of the war period, the Kikuyu Association (KA) was formed. This organisation had a somewhat intellectual and conservative flavour and was concerned chiefly with applying pressure within the law to moderate and review colonial policy as it affected blacks in general and the Kikuyu in particular. This, of course, was primarily in the matter of land. For its part the white settler community remained up until the very end of colonial rule in absolute denial that any such land-based agenda ever existed.

The Kikuyu Association was superseded soon after its formation by the East African Association (EAA), proscribed by the authorities in 1922, and then two years later by the Kikuyu Central Association (KCA). The KCA represented something of a sea change in the black political mindset, inasmuch as its membership tended to be younger, poorer, less educated and significantly more militant. All these organisations, nevertheless, were simply pressure groups. It was the Kenya African Union (KAU), however, formed initially in 1944 as the Kenya African Studies Union that represented the first attempted organisation of an indigenous political party. It was as president of this organisation that veteran Kikuyu activist and spokesman Jomo Kenyatta set in motion the journey of the African peoples of Kenya towards ultimate independence.

Kenyatta was by then a 48-year-old Kikuyu elder who had spent the best part of the previous two decades living in Britain. There he had found himself to be something of a darling of the left wing of the Labour Party and other liberal/intellectual organisations where anti-imperialism was a popular platform. He had furnished himself with respectable credentials through the publication of his book, *Facing Mount Kenya*, as well as by the weight of his personality and intellect, upon all of which he assumed the moral leadership of African nationalism in Kenya. This he did with a determination to create from the movement a fully representative, pan-tribal movement that could speak with authority for all natives of the colony.

He also, interestingly, tended to keep the militant black factions of the Nairobi townships and the emerging Mau Mau movement somewhat at arm's length. He was a skilful orator, and through his use of the Kikuyu tongue, a language founded on allegory, he was able throughout to maintain his nationalist position by neither advocating violence nor explicitly forswearing it. Kenyatta's vision of the future embraced far more than just the short-term concerns of the landless and the plight of the urban unemployed. He in fact found Mau Mau, when it came to the fore of Kenyan politics, to be something of a hot potato. Too close an association with such an overtly violent and atavistic movement as this would obviously have invited all kinds of unwanted attention from the authorities and caused those among his advocates in Britain to question the true depth of his moral certitude. Besides this a slow walk to a British gallows was not how Kenyatta intended to personally influence the direction of the revolution.

Despite this, Kenyatta's 1946 return to the land of his birth prompted huge celebrations among the Kikuyu and much hand-wringing and anxiety among the settlers and administrative offices of native affairs and law and order. According to F.D. Corfield, who wrote the official report on Mau Mau, *Origins and Growth of the Mau Mau*: 'Jomo Kenyatta was adept in the art of appearing not unreasonable in public, while fomenting agitation in secret.'

And evidence of that agitation was never far from those with an interest in taking note of it. According to Fred Majdalany, whose writing tended to define the Mau Mau phenomenon in a manner very palatable to the white settler community, the Kikuyu population in 1945 had never been more prosperous, productive and content, and were it not for Kenyatta's return to the colony matters would have thus remained. However, the moment that the veteran leader did set foot back in Kenya, government land-husbandry policies were resisted, disruptive political activity became commonplace while morale and discipline in the rural areas collapsed.[9]

In fact the increase in violence at that moment was probably coincidental to Kenyatta's return, responding more acutely to the overall political awareness of the Kikuyu and efforts on the part of the Central Committee of the KAU, the *Muhimu*, to forge unity among the various Kikuyu groups through a widespread system of oathing.

The matter of oathing has always been central to historic accounts of the rise of the Mau Mau, and in many ways provided ammunition to the detractors of the movement who wished it to be portrayed as a destructive reversion to savage customs of the past. Lurid accounts saturated the popular media in Britain and beyond of bestial practices and obscene ritual forced on otherwise loyal but susceptible Kikuyu. The truth of the matter is perhaps more prosaic. There certainly was a sensational aspect to the oathing rituals, all of which grew more extreme as the movement administering them did, but at its most basic the oath was merely a system of politicising and conditioning the masses for rebellion in a manner that is widely understood and accepted. Although Mau Mau emerged at a time prior to Cold War brinkmanship in Africa, and the proliferation of Maoist dogma in the matter of developing revolution, the concept of engaging the masses as an essential precursor to armed resistance was understood. It was conducted not through communist ideological brainwashing, however, but through a deeply traditional system of social bonding that, although it might have revolted the British, was rich with meaning and symbolism to the Kikuyu.

Oathing, coupled with amplified anger and grievance, provided the organisational cohesion necessary for a grassroots movement to come into being. Throughout 1948, intelligence reports, based for the most part on rumour that a secret society had begun to coalesce among militant Kikuyu, began to be taken notice of by a traditionally small but alert intelligence community. In September of that year an intelligence report compiled by Special Branch reached the desk of the Member for Law and Order, a local equivalent of the British Home Secretary, that made explicit use for the first time of the name Mau Mau in connection to a new movement, believed to be a branch of the KCA, that had made an appearance in Naivasha, capital of the Rift Valley Province. The name had been circulating anecdotally for some time prior to this, but this was the first time that it appeared in an official report.

The origins of the term Mau Mau remain obscure. It is not an accepted term in any local indigenous language – an escarpment running along the western edge of the Great Rift Valley is known as the Mau Escarpment, with an associated forest system known as the Mau Forest, neither of which conform to areas traditionally inhabited by the Kikuyu – and according to authoritative inside accounts, the name was not commonly used by the militant movement itself other than in its communication with the authorities, who were primarily responsible for adopting and formalising it.[1] The guerrilla groups themselves made reference to their movement only as the Land Freedom Army/Armies or the Freedom Struggle Association.[10] Much later an unrelated and opportunist Swahili acronym, *Mazungu Aende Ulaya, MwaAfrika Apate Uhuru*, was adopted. This translated into 'Let the European go back home, let the African regain Independence'.[11]

Towards the end of 1948, notice also began to be taken of the fact that firearm theft in the colony was increasing in frequency, leading to the obvious conclusion that the natives were arming themselves. In January 1949 it was discovered that some 32,000 rounds of ammunition were missing from the Command Ammunition Depot situated in Gilgil in the Rift Valley Province. A month later it was noted that a further 40,000 rounds were missing from the same location. Much of this was due to lax security, but the fact that such a large quantity of ordnance was now circulating underground became a source of acute concern for the local military and civil authorities.

An orchestrated accumulation of arms was indeed underway, but with as yet no cohesive military plan to guide it, nor any particular manifesto or guiding political philosophy to define it. Besides this, there were in reality too few firearms to mount a meaningful armed struggle. Another crucial factor was that no real source of outside supply existed, which combined with the fact that all the borders of Kenya were secure, meaning that any kind of ambition towards an orchestrated, 1960/70s'-style liberation struggle would be frustrated from the onset.

Violence was nonetheless widespread. An outbreak of arson in the Rift Valley Province began in February 1952, following on from months of intelligence leakages and rumours of illegal meetings and underground mobilisation. The first fighters found their way into the forests of the Central Province in August 1952 under the command of Waruhiu Itote, later to be more widely known as General China.

As the year progressed political agitation and violence increased dramatically, this thanks to a number of key developments. The first was the departure from the colony of the Governor Sir Philip Mitchell, who had brought upon himself the displeasure of the settler lobby by refusing to acknowledge the unrest in Kikuyuland as anything more than a sectarian disturbance affecting a minority of the black population. He was replaced soon afterwards by Sir Evelyn Baring who recognised immediately that matters were a great deal more serious than this. One of Baring's first official duties upon arrival in Kenya was to attend the funeral of Chief Waruhiu, a pillar of the loyalist Kikuyu community, who had

[1] The Colonial Government outlawed an organisation known as 'Mau Mau' in August 1950 and thereafter made reference to all violent political activity under this term.

been murdered in a well-orchestrated Mau Mau operation. The Governor needed little convincing to seek authorisation from Whitehall for a State of Emergency, coming into effect at midnight on 20/21 October 1952. The next day another prominent loyalist chief, Chief Nderi, was murdered at the hands of Mau Mau.

The Government's first response was to mount Operation *Jock Scott*, during which all of the principal political and community leaders, all Kikuyu, and most notably Jomo Kenyatta, were rounded up and detained. After a carefully managed trial, many have since said show-trial, Kenyatta was convicted, alongside his colleagues, and sentenced to a term of seven years imprisonment with hard labour, to be followed immediately afterwards by a period of indefinite restriction.

This, while it might in fact have suited Kenyatta in the short term, shielding him from any direct involvement with and responsibility for Mau Mau, was precisely the sort of high-handed and reactionary response that tended to mark the white settler community in Kenya with such a reputation for racism, and perhaps even fanaticism. Ironically, this reputation bothered even some of those from elsewhere in British Africa, few of whom where ever mistaken for liberals themselves. The net effect, however, was to remove the moderate black element from the process which in turn severed any meaningful line of communication between the races, reinforcing the black view of things, and tending to confirm in the minds of most in the militant movement that whites were greedy, obdurate and uncompromising.

It was also widely appreciated that the administration in Nairobi was corrupt. Much of this corruption was fiduciary, but much was political too. While it would be too much to say that Kenyatta's trial was rigged, there was nonetheless much irregularity in the gathering and presentation of evidence, in the venue, and in the choice of trial judge. This, however, was very much in keeping with how things got done in Kenya at that time.[2]

[2] General Erskine, Forces Commander in Kenya during the Emergency, famously remarked in a letter to his wife that Kenya was "a sunny land for shady people". This, of course, was from the acid quip attributed to W. Somerset Maugham regarding his view of Monaco.

CHAPTER ONE:
IN SUPPORT OF THE CIVIL AUTHORITY

"The mood and temper of the public with regards to the treatment of crime and criminals is one of the most unfailing tests of the civilisation of any country"
—*Winston Churchill*, Commons debate

The Mau Mau Rebellion never achieved the status of a war, civil or otherwise, and was dealt with almost entirely through the application of common law. Emergency regulations provided for the use and aid of the military without usurping overall civilian authority in the containment of the crisis. Therefore, arguably, the most potent and widely applied weapon in the British arsenal was the gallows. Those acts of violence identifiable as being politically motivated, or perpetrated in the furtherance of a military goal, were dealt with through the court system using criminal law with the application thereafter of criminal punishment. No accommodation was made to modern conventions of warfare and no captives afforded the status of prisoner of war. It might be added that many among the settler community saw this as fair and proper treatment for criminals, bearing in mind their refusal to grant the rebellion any status other than criminal, and bearing in mind also that the level of violence perpetrated by Mau Mau, and the manner in which so many victims were killed, exceeded any modern convention of wartime behaviour.[3]

[3] The killing on the evening of 24 January of the Ruck family, and the capture and burying alive of farmer Gray Leakey in October 1954, magnified many times the horror of the situation as it appeared to whites. More blacks than whites by far were hideously murdered during the episode, but the hacking to death with a *simi*, a machete-like utility knife in wide use across central Africa, created such terrible injuries, and implied such an horrific manner of death, that whites recoiled, and reacted with exaggerated demands that the perpetrators be subject to the most extreme penalties of law.

Military units were only entitled to open fire without challenge in areas of forest or mountain known to be uninhabited. These were in due course classified as Prohibited Areas and came to include most of the Aberdare and Mount Kenya forest reserves and surrounding areas, which accounted for the main areas of refuge for active Mau Mau gangs. The Prohibited Area also included a strip several hundred metres wide on the leading edges of both the Aberdare and Mount Kenya forests, each of which were secured by police posts, army camps and patrols. Men captured or detained anywhere within or around these areas were delivered immediately to the police who would seek a conviction based on a transgression of the colony's law. Trials were arbitrated by magistrates with Supreme Court powers, acting under emergency regulations, hearing cases arising from arson, oath administration, murder and assault. In due course, emergency assize courts were introduced, along with the removal of a preliminary hearing prior to appearance before the Supreme Court, in order to deal with the mounting backlog of trials.

An interesting anecdote recorded by Military Intelligence Officer Frank Kitson, in his memoir *Gangs and Counter Gangs*, gives some insight into how difficult and confusing it could be to operate under these conditions:

> One evening Eric Holyoak contacted a small gang, killing one member of it and capturing two others, one of whom had a rifle. The police charged him with being an armed terrorist, the other was charged with consorting. The defence case for the first man was that he had recently been captured by the gang and had been forced to carry the weapon so as to compromise himself. The judge accepted that view and the man was acquitted. Now if this man was not an armed terrorist,

Frank Kitson, who pioneered the 'pseudo' concept.

then the other could not have been consorting with an armed terrorist, so he was acquitted too. All this may have been good law but made little sense to Eric who in addition to the action had also spent some time hanging around in Nairobi waiting to give evidence.[12]

Detention orders were another key element of emergency regulations, allowing for the mass imprisonment of many thousands of Kikuyu for both preventative and screening purposes. The single greatest frustration felt by security forces was their inability to determine from outward appearances the political loyalties of a uniform black population. In this regard intelligence played a key role from the onset. Pivotal would be the hearts and minds concept, introduced into the counter-insurgency lexicon by General Sir Gerald Templar, High Commissioner for Malaya, who commented on the question thus: "... the answer lies not in pouring more troops into the jungle, but rests in the hearts and minds of the people. Winning 'hearts and minds' requires understanding the local culture."[13]

A constable savagely hacked to death by Mau Mau in the charge office of Naivasha police station, 26 March 1952.

Masai tribesmen recruited by settlers as farm guards. Issued with a shotgun and an old greatcoat they patrolled cattle *bomas*, wheat stores and squatter labour lines.

In fact, during the early stages black commitment to the rebellion was almost absolute, with the only exception being a conservative minority of Kikuyu society: those aligned to the government either through appointment as chiefs or through work in the civil services, and those among the Kikuyu who had, through the machinations of land tenure as defined by colonial law, managed to gain land and influence, and who saw no merit in adjusting the status quo. Of these a good many met their ends at the sharp end of a *simi*, or through arson. It was the responsibility of the intelligence community, and most specifically the police Special Branch, to cut through the wall of silence in order to create a three-dimensional picture of the rebellion.

Police Special Branch had from the onset given the administration repeated warnings that trouble was brewing. That nothing at the time was done is more reflective of the Governor's unwillingness to confront reality than any failings in the normal civil early-warning system. This intelligence tripwire, as was typically the case throughout British Africa, had its roots in provincial and district administration and law enforcement, and reached through a network of local informers right down to the grassroots village level.

The local intelligence community, however, was at the time small and ill equipped for the sudden demands of a full-scale insurrection. In November 1952, and again in April 1953, the head of MI5, the British internal intelligence and security organisation, visited Kenya in order to advise on and facilitate the expansion of the colony's security services. Organisational changes included the appointment of a British Security Service official as intelligence adviser to the colonial government along with the rapid expansion in manpower and funding of Special Branch. For specific military intelligence – that which was concerned with combat operations – the post of Senior Intelligence Staff Officer was established at GHQ, with a staff initially made up of plain-clothed police officers deployed in each of the affected areas. In due course these were supplemented by Field Intelligence Assistants drawn from senior NCOs of the Kenya Regiment, all of whom would have been local whites.

In mid-1953, the system was bolstered by the addition of two District Military Intelligence Officers in a supervisory role, both of whom were regular British Army officers. One of these was Captain Frank Kitson who would in due course achieve wide recognition for his work with pseudo groups and the operational use of turned guerrillas.

By the end of 1953, the local intelligence community could confidently claim to have constructed a reasonably accurate picture of the overall organisation and the leading personalities of Mau Mau. This picture came into even sharper focus with the capture on 15 January 1954 of Waruhiu Itote, or General China, one of the original and most influential of the Mau Mau leaders. This event would in fact have a profound effect on the general intelligence picture of Mau Mau, and the military and police special operations tactics that would rapidly begin to evolve to destroy it.

Of the role of the Kenya Police during the Mau Mau Rebellion much has been written, and a general consensus has been reached that the conduct of this force, alongside the Kenya Police Reserve and the Kenya Regiment, left much to be desired. Most of the many reported instances of abuse or mistreatment of captured Mau Mau, suspected Mau Mau or local Kikuyu tribesmen suspected of Mau Mau sympathies, were traceable in one way or another to members of these three units. The anecdotal record in this regard is huge, the official record somewhat smaller, but the fact that a substrata of abusive, vengeful and at times homicidal personnel existed within the Kenya Police and Police Reserve has never been disputed. A British conscript serving with the Devons & Buffs commented during an interview conducted much later: "The Police just treated the prisoners like animals. As soon as you handed them over the kicks and slaps began. Goodness knows what they did to the poor buggers when they got them behind closed doors."[14]

Mau Mau historian, Robert B. Edgerton, in his book *Mau Mau, An African Crucible*, quotes an anonymous interview dated 1962 with a member of the Kenya Police Reserve in reference to the treatment of Mau Mau suspects. Sections of this bear quoting in full:

> ... while we were waiting for the sub-inspector to come back I decided to question the Mickeys.[4] They wouldn't say a thing, of course, and one of them, a coal-black bastard, kept grinning at me, real insolent. I slapped him hard, but he kept on grinning at me, so I kicked him in the balls as hard as I could. He went down in a heap but when he finally got up on his feet he grinned at me again, and I snapped, I really did. I stuck my revolver right in his grinning mouth ... and I pulled the trigger. His brains went all over the side of the Police Station. The other two Mickeys were standing there looking blank. I said to them that if they didn't tell me where to find the rest of the gang I'd kill them too. They didn't say a word so I shot them both. When the sub-inspector drove up, I told him that the Mickeys tried to escape. He didn't believe me but all he said was "bury them and see the wall is cleaned up".[15]

The Kenya Police Reserve and the Kenya Regiment were manned by the compulsory conscription of white males in the colony mandated by the National Service Act, gazetted by the local Legislative Council in 1943. In the matter of human rights abuses, a distinction has been clearly drawn between personnel recruited directly from Britain to augment local police enrolment and those drawn from within the colony for territorial service with either the Kenya Police Reserve or the Kenya Regiment. Conscripted British troops brought in from the outside alongside short contract British police recruits were not so directly vested in the outcome of the rebellion, as were local whites whose commercial and agricultural interests, not to mention matters of personal security, were directly on the line.

This, however, can only be viewed as part of the explanation. The wider conclusion might perhaps have more to do with the moral condition of the white settler community in general. Anecdotal reference to this has been made in frequent accounts of the period, and although it can hardly be defined in terms of specifics, some light can be shed on the matter by the attitudes and observances of those on the outside looking in. One of the most reliable of these must be General Sir George Erskine, of whom much will be heard later, who arrived in the colony in 1953 as GOC-in-Chief of East Africa Command, and who, in frequent letters to his wife, derided the white settler community as being in the main dishonest, racist, violent and undeserving of either the general race-superiority that they awarded themselves or the responsibility to govern.

It must also be reiterated that the conduct of the Kenya Emergency, for all intents and purposes a civil war, was undertaken at all times within the limitations of common law. Subject to these limitations was British Intelligence Officer Frank Kitson:

> And so it came about that, once in a way, somebody would take the law into his own hands and strike a blow where one seemed necessary, because the existing legal methods of dealing with the situation were not good enough. Looking back, I am sure that this was wrong. Certainly this sort of conduct saved countless loyalist lives and shortened the Emergency. All the same it was wrong because the good name of Britain was being lost for the sake of saving a few thousand Africans and a few million pounds of the taxpayers' money. Regardless of their popularity, the leaders of the Government and Security Forces stood four square against such practices, which were anyhow very rare.[16]

Kitson clearly glosses over some of the grosser aspects of mistreatment meted out to Mau Mau suspects, and those detained on active operations, but he also speaks for the obvious frustrations of those trying to do a very difficult job under highly restrictive political conditions. Kitson also observes, quite accurately, that it was not beyond Mau Mau, and Mau Mau supporters within and without the colony, to generate a maximum of effect from these instances, as the many detractors of the organisation did in regards to moments of extreme Mau Mau brutality.

There were also, of course, daily instances of bending the rules. A particular incident recorded by Frank Kitson involved a Kenyan-born Field Intelligence Officer who was building a new operations camp with neither funds nor labour. A raid was

[4] 'Micks' or 'Mickeys' were commonly used vernacular terms to describe Mau Mau, drawn from Mickey Mouse, which referred to the double M in the name Mau Mau. This in turn refers to a long-standing military tradition that includes the ubiquitous 'Jerries' during the Second World War, 'Charlie' and 'Dinks' during the Vietnam War, 'Skinnies' during the US intervention in Somalia, and many others.

General Sir George Erskine, Commander-in-Chief East Africa 1953–59, touring a settler farmer's *shamba* on the Kinangop plateau. Note the pistol slung from the lady's waist.

White children pose in front of their farmstead, typically fortified with barbed wire and sandbags.

therefore contrived on a nearby settlement during a Sunday beer drink, and while a large number of men waited in the camp yard for their papers to be processed, something that could be expected to take all day, the men were put to work building and thatching huts.

Another shrewd use of black expertise and labour was in the formation of the Home Guard, or the Kikuyu Guard, one of the most divisive and yet productive pillars of the British counter-insurgency response. The movement was begun by the Christian missions and senior Christian chiefs of Kikuyuland as protection from attacks mounted against the loyal population by Mau Mau. Loose vigilante and resistance groups began to be formed during the course of 1951, but were not banded together as an organised militia until the suggestion was mooted at an official level sometime towards the end of 1952. The principal motivation for the government in this regard was political: the use of a Kikuyu militia to confront a Kikuyu rebellion would smudge the hitherto clear lines of race conflict, and present the crisis as a black-on-black affair and less as a movement seeking the removal of white minority rule. The official adoption and organisation of a Kikuyu defence system, the Kikuyu Guard, in actual fact set the stage for what could hardly have been less than a civil war. However, it was an astute move, without doubt, and very much in keeping with the divide-and-rule tactics applied elsewhere in British Africa.

The term Home Guard, meanwhile, obviously made reference to the British Second World War version of the same thing, with some scholars now preferring the term Kikuyu Guard, or Kikuyu Resistance. Neither of these terms, however, is popular with the modern Kenyan perception of the matter. This is bearing in mind that resistance implies tyranny, which in turn darkens the legacy of the Mau Mau, which for reasons of liberation mythology has been sanitised somewhat and broadened far beyond its original scope and effect. The Home Guard, nonetheless, remains a practical fact of history, exemplifying by its existence the fact that support for Mau Mau was *not* universal among the Kikuyu, even if dislike and distrust of colonial rule probably was.

The Home Guard was at first placed under the command and control of loyal chiefs who were granted an honorarium, initially of 15 shillings a month, for recruiting and coordinating units in their areas.[17] To begin with these were armed with traditional weapons, perhaps with the addition of a shotgun here and there, although later numbers of precision weapons – unusually the venerable SMLE Lee Enfield rifles that were in wide circulation, but occasionally also automatic weapons – were distributed. The movement was popular among loyalist chiefs, but not universally so. Those, however, with reservations about such an overtly loyalist statement had little choice but to comply, for in fact to demur over the formation of a Home Guard unit would immediately imply loyalty to Mau Mau with all the complications that this would in due course present.

By the end of 1952, Home Guard units had been formed and were active in all the main towns and locations of the White Highlands and within the chieftaincies of the Kikuyu reserve. A year later, in March 1954, it was estimated that there were upwards of 25,000 Kikuyu men associated in one way or another with the Home Guard, with just fewer than 15,000 of these full-time, a number that by then exceeded the total strength of the Land Freedom Armies active within the forests. There were four categories of recruitment to the Home Guard identified: those loyal to the colonial government, those concerned at the perversion of traditional Kikuyu values, those alert to opportunity and those who were Christian.

One of the immediate effects of the arming and support of the Kikuyu defence units was a tilt in the general balance of fortune very much in their favour. In the first instances local scores were settled and land disputes resolved, after which opportunities for racketeering and corruption were seeded which grew quickly into an increasingly comfortable acquisition of wealth. Many of the abuses later unearthed as a consequence of the Emergency – many but by no means all – were perpetrated by the Home Guard in the practice of arbitrary detentions and *ad hoc* interrogations. However, local knowledge counted for much, such that by the end of the Emergency the Home Guard was credited with killing 4,686 Mau Mau, some 48 per cent of the total.[18]

The most important contribution made to the eventual suppression of the Mau Mau by the Home Guard was to deny the rebels supremacy in the Kikuyu reserves. In due course, as the balance

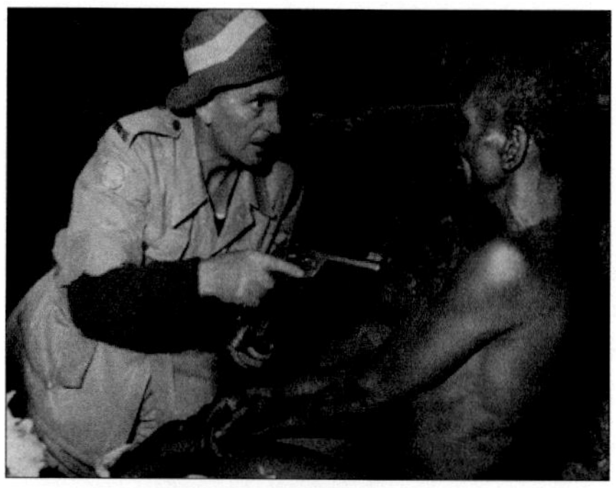

The British were later accused of excessive interrogation techniques.

Jomo Kenyatta in iconic garb, seen after the Mau Mau uprising.

tipped and Mau Mau defeat became inevitable, a critical mass of popular opinion was reached, that although never pro-white, was certainly anti-Mau Mau. This critical mass put the Mau Mau on the defensive, reducing their activities in the end to the meanest of bush survival in the forests and moorland of the highlands, with no discernible military advance made in any direction at all.

Alongside all this was the British military complement requested by Governor Baring as part of the emergency response triggered by the declaration of a State of Emergency. By May the following year the purely military force deployed in the colony included two brigades: 39 Brigade, comprising two, sometimes three battalions of British troops, and 70 Brigade, including five, but sometimes six battalions of the King's African Rifles; included also was the Kenya Regiment, an armoured car squadron, an artillery battery and two RAF squadrons. In September 1953 a second overseas brigade, 49 Brigade was introduced.

The RAF was used primarily on bombing raids over the forested redoubts of the Mau Mau, to very questionable effect, details of which will later be examined. The armoured cars and artillery detachments were deployed principally in the open country between the two main forest reserves, while the KAR battalions served mainly within Kikuyuland or in the white settled areas surrounding the reserves, undertaking methodical clearance operations. The two British brigades, less one battalion that remained in Nairobi, were engaged in intensive patrolling in and around the Prohibited Areas, including for the purpose the forest reserves and adjacent areas, which again had limited effect initially, but which gained effectiveness later as the troops involved found their feet and achieved some proficiency. A close liaison was maintained at all times with the police in the matter of ground coverage, bearing in mind the fact that the entire episode remained classified as a civil disturbance, with no compromise at all made to wartime rules of engagement.

British units were rotated throughout the period of the Emergency, but included at various times the Lancashire Fusiliers, the Gloucester Regiment, the Rifle Brigade, the King's Own Light Infantry, the Black Watch, the Royal Engineers (employed most fruitfully in constructing roads into the forests), the Devons & Buffs, the Royal Northumberland Fusiliers, the Oxford and Buckinghamshire Light Infantry and of course the Royal Air Force.

CHAPTER TWO:

THE LAND FREEDOM ARMIES

> "Perhaps the greatest problem which the Security Forces faced was how to deal with Mau Mau without breaking the law. A full scale civil war was going on around us but the law of the country was still in force and the government was still enforcing it"
>
> —*Frank Kitson*

The advent of a State of Emergency in Kenya came prematurely as far as the *Muhimu* (the Central Committee of the KAU) was concerned, forcing the adoption of armed resistance before any kind of coherent military plan could be developed. Preparations after a fashion had been ongoing for some time, beginning with the appointment of Stanley Mathenge, a military veteran of the Burma Campaign of the Second World War, and leader of a militant black veterans' organisation known as the Forty Group, to oversee military operations, confined largely at that time to the nefarious accumulation of weapons.

Militarily, Mau Mau was never an army in the true sense of the word. The Kikuyu had no military tradition as such, and no outside influence or advice to call upon to compensate for this fact. As a traditionally pastoral and agricultural people the Kikuyu could hardly challenge their close neighbours, the Masai, for age-old military customs and lore, and any inter-clan conflict that might have occurred among Kikuyu and related groups, such as the Embu or Meru, would rarely have amounted to more than armed skirmishes undertaken by militant gangs coalescing briefly and for a specific purpose. Such, in many respects, was Mau Mau.

General China, as we have heard, was the first to enter the forests following a police clampdown on the *Muhimu* in the Nyeri District. He was accompanied initially by only some 30 followers, but numbers swelled rapidly as the Emergency began to take effect. Like Stanley Mathenge, China was a veteran of the King's African Rifles Burma deployment, achieving the rank of corporal in formal military parlance, but awarding himself the rank of general upon taking command of the first wave of Mau

Farm militia lead white farmers on the search for missing livestock.

A British cartoon depicting the white settler sentiment of the time.

The British Colonial Secretary, Alex Lennox-Boyd (with trilby) inspects a Kikuyu Home Guard unit.

Mau recruits. This is in itself indicative of the *ad hoc* development of the movement. The Mau Mau ranking system was obviously fairly arbitrary, with a proliferation of colonels, generals and brigadiers, but with very few if any troopers or privates. The high command included a handful of field marshals, while one prime minister was recorded in the person of Dedan Kimathi, a substantive guerrilla leader, and later the symbolic figurehead of the revolution.

Some ridicule has been applied by unsympathetic writers to this innocent and rather ill-informed interpretation of formal military rank, but, apart from clearly illustrating the naivety and lack of worldly understanding on the part of a largely illiterate movement, this was probably as good a rank structure as any, and it worked well within the very loose organisational structure of Mau Mau.

In the meanwhile, and before we embark on an examination of Mau Mau organisation and structure, a brief note on the nature of the Mount Kenya and Aberdare forests might be useful. A quick glance at a topographical map of Kenya will reveal that the highest point of the country is the snow-capped massif of Mount Kenya. Some 60 miles east of this lies the less definable but no less dramatic Aberdare mountain range that runs south to north for some 80 miles. In between these two highland features lies the Central Province, that which in years past was both the White Highlands and Kikuyuland, and the setting for much of the action that took place during the Mau Mau Rebellion.

Arguably, the principal feature of both of these highland regions remains the belt of tropical mountain forest that skirts each. African tropical highland habitats such as Mount Kenya and the Aberdares, and equally Mount Kilimanjaro to the south and the Rwenzori Mountains to the west, all to a greater or lesser extent conform to a similar ecological structure. Each range owes its existence to the formation of the Great Rift Valley and the volcanic activity that accompanied that. Each rises out of the signature savannah plains or steppe of East Africa, with, at a certain point, a belt of dense forest forming a skirt that is topped at higher altitude by a ring of bamboo, followed by vast landscapes of moorland identifiable as being tropical only upon examination of the diversity of life that it supports. While similarly structured to the rain forest of such regions as the Congo Basin, the highland forests of central and east Africa support a different habitat and a very different climate. Rain is ubiquitous, of course, but the term cloud forest tends to imply much atmospheric moisture too, and indeed a feature of the forests is the clear, fast-flowing, rain-fed rivers that tumble down the steep inclines and through deep-cut gorges. It is these that render the landscapes as awesomely beautiful as they are difficult to navigate and traverse, and certainly the whole eco-system provides a perfect location for large numbers of fugitives to take refuge.

The first wave of these, made up mainly of *Muhimu* activists fleeing arrest in the Kikuyu Reserve, arrived in the forest piecemeal, where they tended to unite into loosely scattered and disorganised gangs based primarily on established familial and village ties.

These would later emerge as the hard core of the movement, many of whom would be among those who would fight to the last. Behind them came large numbers of people who were motivated less by the overarching political objectives of Mau Mau than by a simple need to escape mounting police and military pressure in the reserves. In addition to this, as the Kenyatta trial dominated the headlines towards the end of 1952, large numbers of Kikuyu squatters on white farms began to be 'repatriated' to the reserves as suspicion against them took root, and as white commercial farmers began to clear their properties of any blacks that were surplus to their direct labour needs.

At the same time the government began the large-scale 'screening' of Kikuyu in the reserves in order to isolate and identify Mau Mau support. This prompted a second mass wave of arrivals in the forests which swelled the numbers to upwards of 10,000, significantly boosting both the confidence and the operational capacity of Mau Mau, but doing nothing to tighten up its organisation or solidify any kind of central command structure. It has been noted, meanwhile, that many among those that did enter the forest for whatever reason were forced to burn their identity documents, the hated *kipande*, in order to secure their allegiance. Any native found without this vital document would immediately be subject to interrogation and screening, which would in turn ensure a very unpleasant passage through the system.[5]

At this point the movement enjoyed fairly widespread, if not universal support among the Kikuyu of the reserves. The heavy-handed official response did nothing to divert this support, and for a brief period Mau Mau enjoyed a wide scope of opportunity. The movement was fairly cleanly divided between the active and passive wings, the former obviously being those that entered the forest with the intention of joining the militia and taking part supplied the movement through a complex and largely invisible underground communication network.[19] It ought to be noted however that the rapidly energised government intelligence network was never far behind the civilian leadership of Mau Mau, even before any clear sense had been gained of what Mau Mau actually represented in military terms, which tended to keep the central council fluid and mobile and in constant evolution.

Attached to the Central Committee were the War Office and Army HQ, whose chairman, known as Commander-in-Chief, exercised a highly theoretical command of the armed forces. In practice the War Office was more concerned with recruitment and commissariat problems than actual command and control. It was in the nature of Mau Mau, and in some respects its principal weakness, that it tolerated central control very badly. The reason for this can be traced to the very early formation of the armed wing of the movement. The haphazard arrival of so many prospective recruits into the forest and the lack of any coordinated structure to greet and organise them, tended to result in the emergence of disconnected gangs under leaders who would develop separate and mutually incompatible organisational structures, and who would themselves never be able to reconcile to the concept of a central command.

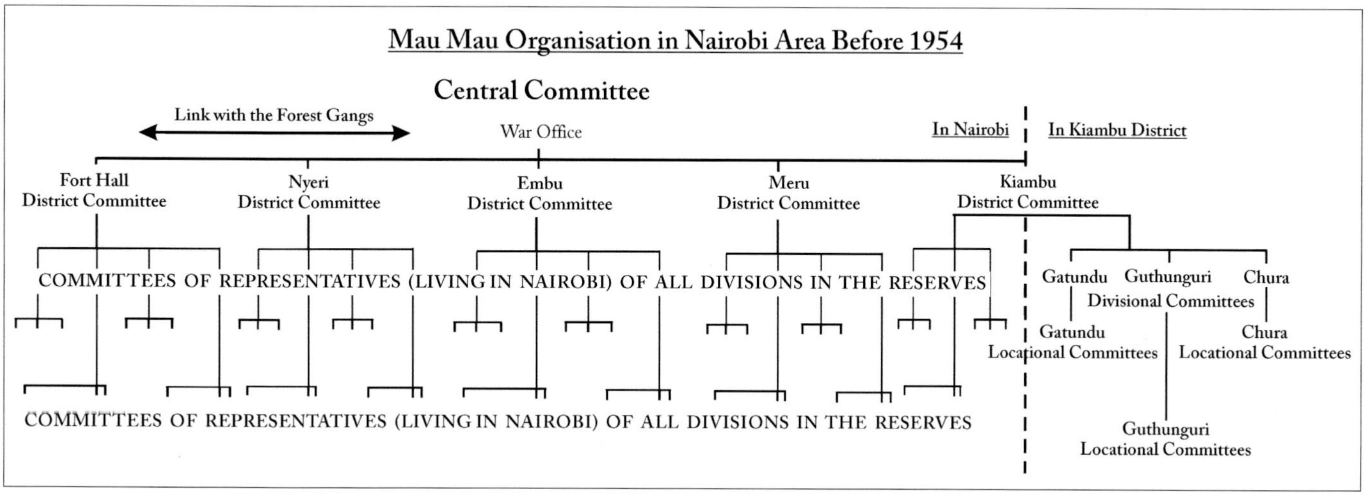

Mau Mau Organisation in Nairobi Area Before 1954

in whatever military strategy might evolve, and the latter being those that had taken some oath of allegiance and were active in a non-combatant capacity in support of the former. This, whether intentional or otherwise, conformed fairly neatly into the communist revolutionary mantra 'the people are like water and the army is like fish' which was recorded by Mao Tse-Tung in his treatise *Aspects of China's Anti-Japanese Struggle* in 1948, and which would come to define the doctrine of a later generation of the Liberation Struggle.

The command structure of Mau Mau in the first phase of its existence was centred in Nairobi where a civilian council, *Kiama kia Miyathi* (Council of Freedom), controlled the activities of and

Within the leadership of the movement three individuals have tended to emerge as the key protagonists. These were General China, who achieved some autonomy as an influential commander of Mau Mau forces in the forests of Mount Kenya and was not particularly challenged in this role, and Stanley Mathenge and Dedan Kimathi, both substantive leaders within the Aberdare forests. There was little practical contact between General China on the one hand and Mathenge and Kimathi on the other, although the latter two did overlap frequently. Despite this, not a moment of genuine cooperation or reconciliation was ever recorded between any of them. The deep and enduring antipathy that each felt for the other arguably inhibited the Mau Mau during its critical phases more than any other factor.

From August 1952 through to about May of 1953, the movement operated, therefore, without any organisational framework at all, wasting a great deal of time and energy on random acts of violence,

[5] The *kipande* was an identity document that recorded specific details such as age, sex, tribe, fingerprints and, most importantly, employment history. The system was designed to limit or moderate the movement of blacks in ostensibly white areas, most urban areas included, and was a common feature of colonial practice across the spectrum.

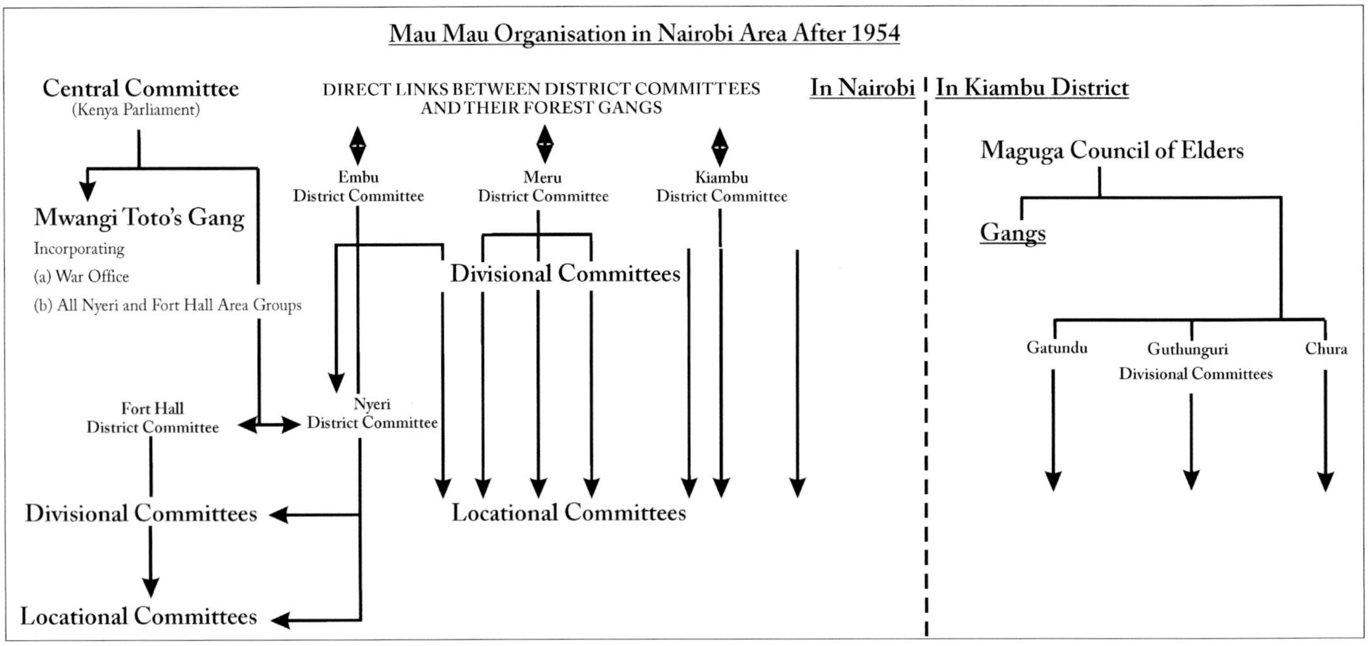

most frequently directed not at whites, but at those Kikuyu perceived as being associated with the Home Guard, or disloyal to the movement in some other way. These attacks, in most cases, were very localised inasmuch as they were informed by events and personalities associated with the villages and home areas from which the members of the responsible gang originated. Quite frequently individual units would be ignorant of the activities of, and often even the existence of, other units operating elsewhere in the forest.

On a tactical and leadership level it can reasonably be argued that the effect of Operation *Jock Scott*, that which removed both Kenyatta and every other substantive nationalist leader from the frame, rendered the movement temporarily headless, even though it was true that none of those detained had in any way been active on the front line.

A noticeable change, however, began to take effect within the movement as it became clear that individual and incongruent groups could not even guarantee their own material survival let alone hope to meaningfully confront the security forces. Larger camp clusters therefore began to form under a more substantive leadership, although still, frustratingly for those few within the movement with a broader tactical vision, the idea of a central command structure remained elusive.

The first concerted effort to overcome the command individualism that had become entrenched in the movement occurred in May 1953 with the formation of the first district-wide (Nyeri District) military unit, the *Utuma Ndemi* Trinity Council, and the *Ituma Ndemi* Army, to which Stanley Mathenge was appointed chairman and head of the armed forces, deputising six substantive camp cluster leaders who were designated 'Generals'. The fly in the ointment, however, was Dedan Kimathi, a precocious, enormously self-absorbed and manifestly unstable character who rose to a command position in the Aberdare chapter of Mau Mau, but who was unable to effect control over the movement as a whole. His contribution was the introduction of the Kenya Defence Council, a similarly high-sounding central control body that again fell afoul of individual leadership ambition, which in the end it merely legitimised by establishing a formal military hierarchy recognising eight independent Land Freedom Armies along with their accepted leadership and their various sectors of operation.

In practical terms, however, Kimathi refused to recognise Mathenge and the *Ituma Ndemi* Army, and vice versa, while General China, largely unchallenged in the forests of Mount Kenya, and already recognised as commanding an individual Land Freedom Army, saw no reason whatsoever why he should recognise or respond to directives from either body – a sentiment echoed by many others besides him.

Kimathi then tried again with the formation in February 1954 of the Kenya Parliament, which, besides attempting to position itself as a political entity in control of the armed wing of the movement, tended to reflect Kimathi's higher ambitions by, rhetorically at least, presenting itself as the civilian party most likely to form a government at the conclusion of what was assumed no doubt would be a successful military campaign. It must be added here, however, for the sake of modifying what might seem from the outside a paralysing quixotic view of the future, that one of the defining premises of the Mau Mau had always been, in a hopeful illusion that can trace its roots as far back as John Brown's raid on the armoury at Harper Ferry, that an incendiary action such as launching a rebellion would incite the masses to revolt in order to overwhelm the administration with the power of a popular revolution.

This, of course, did not happen, but in the meanwhile, and despite the inherent weakness of Mau Mau structure, a credible campaign was fought that not only shed much white and black loyalist blood, and at the cost of millions of pounds to the local and metropolitan treasury, but which ultimately did, if not directly, then certainly indirectly, begin the journey of the nation towards ultimate independence.

CHAPTER THREE:
PARADISE LOST

"It was one of the odd facts of the Kenya Emergency that as soon as a Mau Mau killed a European everything came to a halt while troops, police, CID, and all available senior officers hurried to the scene"
—*Frank Kitson*

The main focus of Mau Mau attrition was the loyalist Kikuyu population. Notwithstanding the high profile removals of loyalist chiefs, and the hitherto rather theoretical threat posed to whites, it had always been, and it remained, the common tribesman of the reserves that felt the main force of Mau Mau activity. This fact remains an enduring irony of just about any guerrilla insurgency or liberation struggle: that the main focus of violence and terror is inwardly turned, against those for whom the struggle is ostensibly aimed, but who might not be, or might not be perceived to be, in perfect ideological alignment to the cause. "Because the guerrillas operated in their home areas," writes Munyabari O Maloba, "they were able to isolate traitors and eliminate them quickly." These killings, Maloba concluded, had a salutary effect on other would-be traitors, and of course, the more horrifying the methods the more complete would be the lesson learned.

The lesson learned by whites, the majority of whom were onlookers absorbing the facts through press reports, victim accounts and imagery, was that Mau Mau was an aberration, a diseased limb on the body of native society that required nothing less than a swift and comprehensive amputation. That the whole matter was so intertwined with witchcraft and mysticism, and solemnised by such abominable and incomprehensible ritual, it was relatively easy to detach it from any justifiable political cause and relegate it to the realm of madness and monstrosity. An example of the kind of language in common use at the time is offered by contemporary Kenyan author Christopher Wilson who wrote a series of short books presaging the fall of white Africa and predicting much that subsequently came to pass.

> The next open outburst of Mau Mau violence took the form of an attack on the cattle and sheep of European farms, when hundreds of wretched animals were slashed and mutilated, to be left in lingering agony. This was a revolting exhibition of African cruelty at its worst ... [F]armers and their wives, even little children, were hacked to death by devils who up to the moment of their black treachery had been treated as loyal and trusted friends.[20]

The targeting of settler livestock was indeed a fact of Mau Mau attacks against the local commercial farming community. What Wilson was probably referring to, however, in the matter of 'little children', was no doubt the shocking incident that took place on 24 January 1953 when 38-year-old Roger Ruck, his pregnant wife Esmé, a doctor who ran a local dispensary, and their six-year-old son Michael were murdered at the hands of a Mau Mau gang. The raw facts of the killings state that Ruck's Kikuyu groom summoned his employer late in the evening with news that a Mau Mau guerrilla had been captured on the farm. Ruck had no reason to distrust his groom who had been in his employ for many years, and who had lately been teaching his son to ride. However, as Peter Hewitt, a British policeman who recorded his own memoirs of the period in a book entitled *Kenya Cowboy*, remarked of the Rucks: "They were, as far as I was concerned, the last [latest] folk on the Kinangop to be caught napping."[21] Ruck left the house and followed the groom towards the farm outbuildings where he was abruptly confronted by an armed Mau Mau gang and cut down in

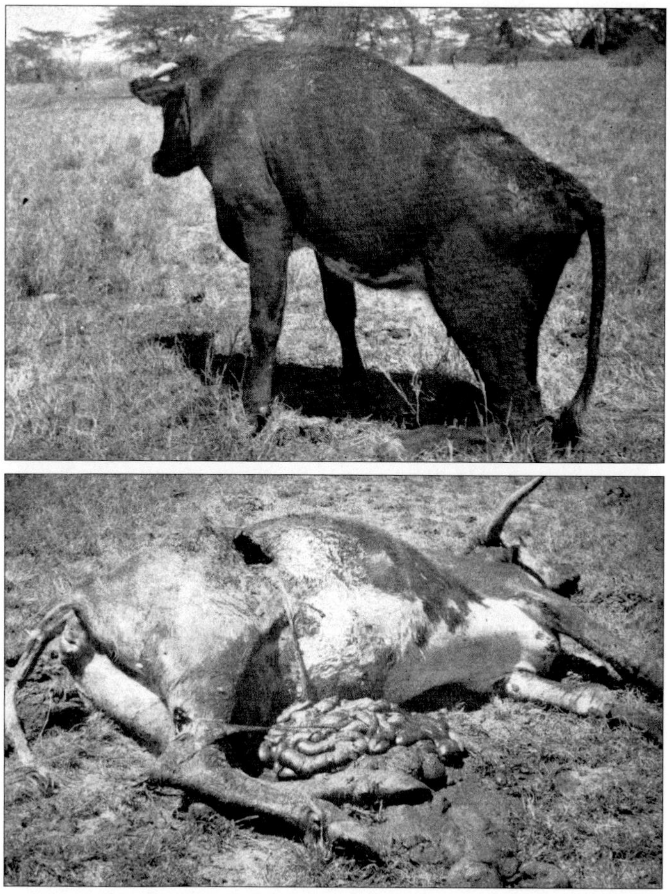

Mau Mau gangs, when thwarted in their raids on cattle *bomas*, would express their anger by cruelly disemboweling or hamstringing the animals denied them.

Mau Mau guerrillas.

Above: The Lari Massacre justifiably presented the British with a wealth of propaganda material.

Left: Following a report of stolen livestock, policeman Peter Hewitt and his men attempt to track down the perpetrators. A herdsman points out spoor of the rustled cattle. *Photo Peter Hewitt*

a frenzy of flailing pangas. Moments later, hearing his cries, Esmé Ruck followed and was similarly cut down. The gang then entered and ransacked the home, finding Michael in bed where he too was hacked to death.

The irony that struck many whites in the aftermath of these bloody murders was the complicity of the family's Kikuyu staff. This fact struck right to the core of the settler self-image – at least the self-image of the majority – who felt that they had throughout treated their local native staff with consummate fairness and equanimity. Indeed, the fact was widely circulated that Esmé Ruck volunteered much time and expertise in the provision of free medical services to local black communities, none of which appeared to impact her fate in the slightest. The killing of young Michael Ruck also seemed unjustifiably barbaric and unnecessary. The whole episode did much to harden the attitudes of local whites, and to lend some credence to the gloomy prognostications, and calls for radical and decisive action against the 'Kukes' by the handful of hawks in the community, whose voices now began to seem more credible, and to be heard with more sympathy.

Peter Hewitt himself recounts a chilling incident that, were it not for the copper's sixth sense that he had acquired as a consequence of several months working in close commerce with his Kikuyu police details, he too would have been one of those caught napping in the Kinangop. Summoned late at night by known and trusted members of the Kikuyu staff of the farm upon which his police post was located, Hewitt left the safety of his quarters and stepped out into the darkness in the company of these men. He was armed, but likewise he was outnumbered. The call-out concerned the supposed theft of grain by Mau Mau which was a frequent-enough occurrence for this to be a credible claim. However, as Hewitt noticed one of his escorts manoeuvring behind him as they walked towards the farm outbuilding, he began to develop an extremely bad feeling. The men surrounding him were each armed with the ubiquitous panga and, although silent, each emanated a nuanced tension that was not lost on the lone white man in their midst. "Then suddenly I was afraid," Hewitt wrote of the episode, "very afraid, though remarkably unembarrassed by such a condition. My Sterling[6] gun felt hard and protective hugged against my hip. Yet I also felt so stupidly impotent against spears and pangas at close quarters."[22]

Hewitt then stopped, and in the darkness placed himself in a position where he could cover all the members of his escort, after which he announced that he was returning to the police post. This he did, ensuring that each man walked ahead of him. Nothing was said and the matter concluded at the door of Hewitt's quarters. The following day it was revealed that no theft of grain had taken place, which tended to place the prior evening's adventure in perspective, and what is more relationships continued without any further reference to the matter. Such was the nature of life, and death, in the Central Highlands. Hewitt celebrated what he believed had been a narrow escape, and thereafter kept a very close eye on all of the blacks in his vicinity, even those that were trained police details.

Many other narrow escapes were recorded, and indeed no small number of Mau Mau died at the hands of settlers fighting back

[6] The Sterling, or Patchett sub-machine gun, was a ubiquitous firearm during operations against Mau Mau in Kenya. Alongside the equally ubiquitous Sten sub-machine gun, it served police, military and pseudo units throughout the Emergency. Both were useful in forest conditions, although in each case the sideways-angled magazine tended to catch in dense undergrowth and cause some problems. Both had interchangeable magazines, the Sten version being straight and the Sterling version being hooked; the latter of course being more prone to entanglement in dense undergrowth.

Senior Kikuyu Chief Njiri, prime mover of the Kikuyu Home Guard. He was murdered by Mau Mau on 6 October 1952, the last of the three senior Kikuyu chiefs to be assassinated.

Sir Evelyn Baring GCMG, KCVO, Governor of Kenya during the Emergency. He became Lord Howick of Glendale. He died in 1973, following a fall down a rock face on his Northumberland estate.

when their homesteads came under attack. One particular incident involved two elderly European women, Kitty Hesselberger and Raynes Simpson, who fortunately had taken to heart police warnings to be alert to strange behaviour on the part of domestic staff and never to stray far from a firearm. Alerted by a house servant's odd behaviour, both women were ready for the first Mau Mau fighter who forced his way into the room, shooting the man dead immediately, with others put to flight by a fusillade of shotgun and pistol fire that, it was later discovered, killed an additional two Mau Mau attackers.

Needless to say, the result of this attack gave heart to a white settler community for the first time coming to terms with the fact that the good days were well and truly over. Over a half-century or more the whites of the Highlands, and elsewhere in Kenya where pockets of Europeans thrived, had gradually but successfully built a comfortable existence for themselves from the raw landscape of east Africa. Those who did not start out with money seldom ended up with much, notwithstanding the overall reputation of white settlers of the region as being pampered, exploitative and self-serving. An inimitable climate and strong fraternal unity tended to compensate for some of the early hardships suffered, until by the latter half of the 20th century the aura of comfortable prosperity that was presented in the White Highlands was regarded as nothing less than what was due to the pioneers as reward for two generations of risk, toil and debt. There was, therefore, a tremendous groundswell of resentment and anger that, no sooner had matters settled into some sort of security and affluence, than the blacks wanted it all handed over to them. And what is more, they had nothing more than gruesome violence to offer in exchange for the 60 years of peace and security they had enjoyed under the *Pax Britannia*, during which time their population had risen to levels inconceivable when the Maasai had roamed the country unhindered, and when slave traders razed the landscape and held the native inhabitants fugitive.

It is hardly surprising, therefore, that the Ruck murders galvanised an immediate and ugly response within the local white community. The fact that the hawks were now in the ascendancy was felt immediately, and not only on the hides of local Kikuyu netted in Nairobi, or in the reserves, or indeed those Mau Mau unfortunate enough to be captured, tried and hanged, but on the Governor himself. Baring woke on the morning after the Ruck murders sensing that this would be a very rough day indeed. That morning, stationed along the roads leading into Nairobi, the Kenya Police Reserve was to be found stopping all vehicles being driven by a European and informing them of a protest meeting to be held at Government House later that morning. By mid-morning a substantial number of whites had already forced their way past the black police details guarding the gates and were spread out on the lawns of the official residence, demanding the immediate appearance of the Governor.

Baring, for his part, had lately begun to wilt in the face of this and other angry criticisms that had been emanating steadily from the local legislature and settler committees across the Central Highlands. From above he had been cautioned to retain the moral authority of the Crown while from below he was heckled constantly for foot dragging and inactivity. Being a man of deep spiritual convictions and in other respects something of a liberal peer with a vacillating character and unsteady constitution, a gathering of belligerent whites pressing a retributional agenda was the last thing he felt able to cope with. Ultimately it was Michael Blundell, leader of the elected members of the legislature, who managed to calm the crowd and persuade them to disperse, promising that Baring would indeed in due course apply himself to sterner measures, and cautioning against whites taking matters into their own hands.

If blacks in the Kikuyuland, meanwhile, considered this spate of white killings, and the hubris it generated, with some circumspection – such things, after all, had been a fact of their lives for some time now – matters were brought very much home to the reserves two months later in what was perhaps the signature Mau Mau operation of the war.

The Lari Massacre was in essence an assault by Kikuyu against Kikuyu, as a majority of Mau Mau actions were, pitching guerrillas against the Home Guard and rebels against loyalists in an episode that would have ramifications deep into the future. The events of the evening of 26 March 1953 began with a brazen and well-executed raid by Mau Mau against an isolated police post in the Naivasha Province, resulting in the deaths of two native police details and the release of some 150 prisoners, but perhaps most importantly, in the seizure of a large quantity of firearms and ammunition. Later that evening a Mau Mau force descended on the northern Kiambu settlement of Lari where they set about the carefully planned massacre of suspected loyalists, culminating in the death of Chief Luka wa Kahangara, a leading loyalist and Home Guard promoter. Most, if not all known non-loyalists were spared, or spared at least by the Mau Mau, for the Home Guard, no doubt enraged by the attacks, exacted prompt and no less violent and bloody reprisals against suspected Mau Mau sympathisers, with the final death toll of the evening recorded at ninety-seven.

The following morning, as the sun rose on the confused and bloody aftermath, the scene recorded by the press and presented to the outside world was largely shown as the actions of the Mau Mau. The resultant propaganda coup was deeply satisfying for a government and public hungry for confirmation of the savagery that they daily confronted. This, it would later transpire, marked a turning point in the all-important battle for hearts and minds that would be so crucial in deciding the ultimate direction of the conflict.

What shocked and surprised many Kikuyu, and indeed no small number of Mau Mau, was the fact that most of the victims had been women and children who had been killed quite often in the most horrific circumstances. From that moment on the majority, no matter what their stance on the wider issues of land distribution and political rights, began to have doubts about the ideology and moral currency of the current conflict. It seemed now to have developed about it the flavour of a vendetta, a settling of scores that had little to do with the progress of the overarching black political agenda. Many analysts have indeed pointed to this as the moment that popular support for the struggle turned a corner.

While never again quite so extreme, the massacre at Lari triggered a concentrated Mau Mau offensive against loyalists and Home Guard across the Kikuyu Reserves. Baring was true to his promise to initiate sterner measures, and, in April 1953, additional legislation was introduced under emergency powers that intensified collective punishment and widened the scope of capital punishment.

That same month the build-up of British troops continued with the arrival in the colony of an additional two battalions, bringing the total to nine.

Not far behind, touching down in Nairobi on 7 June 1953, came General Sir George Erskine, despatched from Britain under the personal endorsement of Prime Minister Winston Churchill, and with authorisation to declare Martial Law should he see fit. His mandate was to assume command of operations against Mau Mau in the colony, assuming a command previously held by Major-General Sir William Hinde, and to bring matters to a speedy and satisfactory conclusion.

CHAPTER FOUR:

THE BLUNT INSTRUMENT

General George Erskine brought with him an injection of energy that was not always matched by enthusiasm for the cause for which he was fighting. He arrived in Kenya with fairly deeply rooted prejudices against the white settler community that were quite unusual for the times, and that appeared to be quickly confirmed by what he found within the colony. His impressions were confidentially recorded in a number of letters written home to his wife, all of which were deeply scathing of the moral value of whites in the colony, and filled with expressions of personal loathing. None of this made it easy for him to merge and interact with local whites, which, in fact, did not seem to bother him much, and indeed, perhaps it was this very distance from the paranoia and emotion of the affair that allowed him to view and assess the situation in a clear and analytical manner.

With, once again, extraordinary perception for the times, Erskine very quickly came to the conclusion that the ultimate solution to the crisis would have to be political. He had no doubt that Mau Mau could be dealt with militarily, but also that this fact, in and of itself, would not represent an end to the affair. "It was at once apparent that the roots of Mau Mau lay very deep in the Kikuyu tribe," he wrote in a retrospective despatch to the Secretary of State for War. "There was almost entire unity of political purpose in the political aims of the Kikuyu, but only a small proportion of the tribe was agreed that these aims could be achieved by force."[23]

Erskine's concern, however, was military and not political, and initially at least he viewed the military situation in clear and simple terms. What was required was the containment, liquidation or capture of somewhere between 12,000 and 15,000 Mau Mau guerrillas operating from internal bases with neither external funding, outside support or the involvement of any other friendly power. The standard of military opposition was also correctly judged to be marginal, and notwithstanding the fact that some among the senior leadership of Mau Mau could claim a degree of military instruction during the Second World War, no organised guerrilla or revolutionary training had been applied to the mass of Mau Mau at all.

Although it represented no particular tactical advantage to Mau Mau in terms of offensive action, the most significant advantage that the movement still enjoyed was the difficulty of the terrain in which the war, such as it was, would be fought. The only British units even vaguely prepared for operations in the highland forests of Kenya were those that had arrived from Malaya where a comparable counter-insurgency campaign was underway. However, the only common feature of the jungles of South East Asia and the forests of the Central Highlands were the

General Sir George Erskine.

Peter Hewitt poses outside his police 'digs' at Hermann's Post, near Gilgil. *Photo Peter Hewitt*

A squad of askari at long last resplendent in uniforms that took many months to arrive at remote forest posts. *Photo Peter Hewitt*

trees. The jungles of Malaya are low lying, fecund, humid and hot. The forests of Mount Kenya and the Aberdares occur at high altitude and are precipitous, bitterly cold during the dry periods and utterly saturated during the rains.

This advantage, however, was only of any value in the matter of remaining hidden. It did not offer easy access to the main economic centres of the colony, in particular once the populated areas surrounding the forests had been secured and cleared, at which point Mau Mau guerrillas tended to become preoccupied less with offensive operations and more with the key issue of survival. Of equal importance was supply, which was in itself premised on the mobilisation of large sectors of the passive wing for the portage of ordnance and food into the forest, and the gathering of operational intelligence for guerrilla forces leaving the forest in order to conduct operations.

Throughout the remainder of 1953, meanwhile, Erskine concentrated on a series of orthodox operations involving ground troops drawn primarily from British battalions, but with KAR elements in support. These operations on the whole took place in and around the Kikuyu reserves and throughout the course of the year reported mixed results. The customary sequence would involve some sort of a hit-and-run Mau Mau attack, or a report of stock theft, after which a combined follow-up would be mounted that would more often than not return little or no result. At this point Mau Mau appeared to have the advantage. A large haul was recorded in April 1953 with the killing by British forces of 24 guerrillas and the capture of 36 others. This, however, tended to be the exception rather than the rule, and was balanced out by rare but nonetheless disturbing incidences, such as that on 13 April 1953 where a follow-up patrol comprising six Europeans and 12 Africans fell afoul of an ambush and suffered three fatalities, all white.[24] According to Peter Hewitt, whose personal account of his period of service in Kenya doing precisely this type of work is rich with incidents of failure, frustration and fruitless misadventure:

> ... the element of risk was seldom considered big enough to inhibit their [Forest Post personnel of the Kenya Police] unremitting search for Mau Mau terrorists in the thickest of tangled jungle and the deepest of gorges. But the locating of actual gangs was a game of chance with the odds stacked against them. Moreover, bumping into a gang while actually on patrol or during a follow-up operation was even more remotely destined to occur.[25]

Here Hewitt touches on a point that does somewhat invite further scrutiny. What could realistically be expected from metropolitan British troops, fresh from the jungles of Sheffield or Leicester, in the pursuit of 'wily Micks' through the darkest recesses of the highland forests of Kenya? How would a domestic animal fare in an equal contest of survival with a wild animal, asked Peter Hewitt? But how, by the same token, can a population of wild animals survive a systematic and scientific extermination.

Initially, before the strategies of extermination had been devised – tactics such as the construction of tracks and roads into the forest, and the development of pseudo gangs to fight fire with fire, British troops, and, in fact, white troops in general, were at a huge disadvantage in any offensive action taken against Mau Mau on their home ground. Mau Mau gangs, on the other hand, were able, largely at will, to leave the forest, enter the reserves or the white farming areas, conduct operations and return to the forest with the highest probability that those stumbling around in pursuit would cross their paths only as a consequence of the most outrageous bad luck. It is also interesting to note the difference in interpretation of this phenomenon from men such as Peter Hewitt and others who have written the history of Mau Mau from the perspective of the guerrillas themselves.

Munyabari O Maloba, for example, makes the very fair point that the Kikuyu were not traditionally forest people, and as a consequence entered the fight with no greater or lesser advantage than any other in the subsequent cat-and-mouse game that would ensue. The Kikuyu were, in fact, during most of their history, rather nervous of the dark and brooding presence of this vast natural eco-system. It was entered only very superficially for the purpose of hunting, usually undertaken using snares, and the harvesting of wild honey. For the remainder the Kikuyu were a pastoral and agricultural people whose preferred habitat

In the corner of the Gilgil police station, an askari takes fingerprints off the corpse of a high-ranking Mau Mau, watched by curious onlookers.
Photo Peter Hewitt

Security forces loading a wounded General China into a vehicle.

General China stands trial at Nyeri. He had commanded all Mau Mau on Mount Kenya. The death sentence was later commuted to life imprisonment as a result of his efforts to organise a general surrender.

was traditionally the open country in between Mount Kenya and the Aberdares, or other areas where their practice of shifting cultivation could be pursued with a minimum of land clearing and pre-preparation.

With this understood, however, it is hard to imagine that individual Mau Mau guerrillas did not approach this uniquely difficult habitat without some advantage over British troops operating in Africa for the first time. Only the most ill-informed or determinedly derogatory European memoirs of the period fail to betray some awe at the proficiency that Mau Mau achieved in the use of their natural environment. Ian Henderson, a denizen of the White Highlands, and a recognised intelligence supremo at the time, was among few whites who spoke Kikuyu, and among even fewer who understood the mindset of this famously abstruse nation. Even he conceded the almost superhuman superiority of Mau Mau operatives moving within the forest environment. To quote Peter Hewitt on the matter again:

> Mau Mau bushcraft and ability to interpret the minutest disturbance of grass or soil was absolutely phenomenal. In an instant the wary 'mick' could decide whether the being that made the mark or disturbance was friend or foe. There was a method, or better still, code, of movement and passage through the forest when in the vicinity of the hide that was practised by Mau Mau and which defied imitation by all except the esoteric.[26]

However, once British troops began to get the feel of the terrain, and once they had begun to avail themselves of local intelligence and support personnel in the form of trackers and informants, successes began to accrue. Three important series of combined operations involving police, army and Home Guard were rolled out between November 1953 and February 1954, accounting for several hundred Mau Mau dead and many key captures. One of these was Waruhiu Itote, the infamous General China, whose cooperation with the government over the next few months in an effort to secure the surrender of the key Mau Mau leader was highly suggestive of a change in the popular view of Mau Mau and its ultimate chances of success.

The RAF, in the meanwhile, commenced bombing operations against Mau Mau in the forests that have to date remained controversial in regard to their overall effectiveness. The RAF itself invested a great deal of time and energy into the air campaign against Mau Mau, and has since had to defend its role against a great deal of professional criticism. There can be no doubt that the 'blind' bombing undertaken upon very vague intelligence tended to inflict very little direct damage on Mau Mau, and nor did it particularly harm enemy morale. In fact, in most cases, the opposite was true. Heavy bombing in the forest had the effect of alerting Mau Mau to the fact that the area was clear of British units which was always a welcomed fact. Moreover, crashed aircraft, of which there were several during the course of the campaign, provided fugitive Mau Mau with a vital source of materials such as wire for snaring and plastic and sheet metal for a multitude of different uses and applications. Another factor that has rarely been written into history, but which impacted British and local troops significantly, was the fact that indiscriminate bombing injured and enraged wild animals such as elephant, rhino and buffalo that in turn took out their anger on hapless army patrols, claiming the lives of no small number of men.

The RAF also applied its resources to the ongoing psyops (psychological operations) in the form of staging sky shouts and the dropping of millions of propaganda pamphlets that undoubtedly did reinforce a negative popular view, and the eventual suppression, of the revolt. At the very least, the image of invincibility that government forces projected was enhanced significantly by the sight of aircraft in constant attendance to the campaign, with the associated general realisation that nothing the Mau Mau could offer by way of resistance would in the long term have any chance against a power of this magnitude.

Arguably it was the Kenya Police Reserve Air Wing that offered the more directly useful service to the prosecution of military operations than the RAF, providing low-key support, eye-in-the-sky-type surveillance, the transport of commanders, special forces or casualties and the dropping of food and supplies into the forest to support patrols on long-range operations.

Such was the nature of military pressure being gradually brought to bear against Mau Mau units in their forest redoubts. In this respect Mau Mau had been checked. Making free with unprotected livestock or unprotected homesteads was one thing, but dealing with a rapidly consolidating counter move by His Majesty's Forces proved a far tougher nut to crack, and, in fact, Mau Mau was solidly checked, if not quite yet put on the defensive.

Erskine, however, recognised one thing very early. The head of the snake was not located in the forests, but in Nairobi. It was there that much of the Mau Mau organisation, coordination and decision-making machinery was to be found. He therefore made severing that head his priority for 1954. To this end Operation *Anvil* was launched on 24 April that year. Lasting a month, it effectively decapitated Mau Mau using the blunt instrument of targeting almost the entire Kikuyu population of Nairobi, which was then exhaustively screened, with individuals further detained if found to be even marginally suspect. In this way many key *Muhimu* leaders, enforcers, organisers and facilitators were swiftly and cleanly removed from the active sphere.

The operation took the form of a comprehensive series of cordons thrown around key areas of the city, making use of units of the police, the KPR and the army. Inspiration was drawn from similar cordon-and-search operations that had achieved reasonable success in Palestine. Once the Kikuyu population had been isolated and contained, four investigating teams were put in place to systematically screen every individual, separating the innocent from the guilty with a very wide mesh indeed. Any person lacking one or all of four specific documents that an individual was required under law to carry, and even a great many who simply seemed likely to be sympathetic to Mau Mau, were rounded up and detained in holding camps strategically positioned on the outskirts of the city.

One aspect of the methodology of screening was the use of the 'hooded man', a simple concept whereby a captured guerrilla or apprehended member of the *Muhimu* hierarchy would be turned for the purpose of identifying others in the movement. These men would be kept in isolation with their identities protected, and then given the opportunity to identify, from a passing parade of detainees, those who were members of or sympathetic to Mau Mau.

Military Intelligence Officer Frank Kitson, in his memoir *Gangs and Counter Gang,* offers a brief description of the hooded men at work:

> About four days after the operation [*Anvil*] started I drove to the main holding camp at Langata on the outskirts of Nairobi to see how things were going. Whilst there I saw a Special Branch officer with three Africans, who were wearing white hoods. They were looking at a long line of suspects and occasionally picking out ones who were then taken aside for questioning. I made some enquiries and discovered that the men in the hoods were themselves high-ranking Mau Mau who had decided to help the Government.[27]

Although ultimately very successful, Operation *Anvil* was nonetheless draconian, impersonal and highly bureaucratic, and it won very few friends for the government among the wider Kikuyu population (although not overtly acknowledged, the operation had quite clearly been surgically aimed at incising suspect Kikuyu out of general circulation). Control over the movement of Kikuyu, and blacks in general, was thereafter consolidated by the introduction of a new passbook system, followed by sustained police and military patrolling throughout the native areas of Nairobi, with regular spot-checking and a steady pressure applied to prevent any resurgence of active political organisation in the capital. Although many innocent, law-abiding individuals did happen to be affected, and a great deal of general harm and inconvenience was caused, the net result was that the active Mau Mau hierarchy, and its complex cells and lines of communications, were effectively dismantled.

The injury to the movement was traumatic, with the effect in the forests being felt almost immediately. Security force pressure, of course, increased tangibly in the main population areas of the Central Highlands, and with such government measures as forced villagisation and the abrupt removal of the Mau Mau central coordinating body, effectively isolated the forest fighters and

British troops on the streets of Nairobi, checking identity papers. Anyone whose papers were not in order was arrested.

British troops watch over locals arrested for questioning in a village.

confined them to their base of operations.[7] Mau Mau operations gradually, although not immediately, began to degenerate and display the character of foraging expeditions aimed at survival and appearing increasingly more desperate and criminal in nature.

In the meanwhile, and as major military preparation was underway to follow up *Anvil* with increased penetration of the forest, a curious encounter was taking place between a policeman and a guerrilla leader that offered hope, very briefly, for an early end to the crisis.

The capture of Waruhiu Itote, otherwise known as General China, had been something of a landmark event, and a great morale boost for the white community that had, up until that point, been rather starved of good news. The obvious propaganda value of such a high-profile capture was eclipsed only slightly by the probable intelligence bonanza if General China could be persuaded to talk. The man tasked with the interrogation was Assistant Superintendent Ian Henderson, of whom we have briefly heard, and who was one of the most able intelligence and operational specialists among the White Highlanders.

Henderson, although born in Scotland, was the son of a pioneer settler and had grown up on a farm in the Nyeri District. Here, in keeping with the experience of a majority of white youth of the time, he roamed freely through a clean and wild landscape, with a rifle in his hand and the fealty of any number of young Kikuyu playmates from the labour lines and villages. (From these boys Henderson was uniquely keen to learn.) He learned to speak the Kikuyu language, which was not by any means widely spoken among whites, and certainly not to the extent that Henderson was able to master it. Perhaps even more important than this, though, in the years that were to come, was the rare fluency that he was able to achieve in Kikuyu culture and social peculiarities. The Hollywood cliché of a white man of Africa was not absent from the self-image of a good many white Kenyan men of the time, but in fact a majority of these were usually only mildly conversant, with men like Henderson, and a very few others, being unique in truly being able to converse with a native Kikuyu speaker with a very clear understanding of the nuances and mindset of the speaker. Louis Leakey was perhaps another of these, although his attributes tended to be scholarly, while Henderson's were instinctual, based on no specific study and informed by no doctrine. A remark by his biographer, Phillip Goodhart, sums this up very well: "He knew both the thickets of the forest and the thickets of the terrorist mind."

This, in combination with a natural cunning and the third eye of a hunter, equipped Henderson perfectly to enter the dark and sometimes seedy world of colonial intelligence and counter-intelligence in one of the dirtiest little campaigns ever fought in the service of the British Empire.

At his point of capture, meanwhile, General China had assumed quite reasonably that he would hang the moment that he had been wrung dry of any useful information. It was also to be assumed that he would be thrown to the Home Guard for the usual rough and unpleasant journey to the gallows. Thus he was extremely pleasantly surprised, and no doubt somewhat disarmed, to be greeted as he waited in a sparse interrogation room by a young, fresh-faced and affable white man who not only addressed him with courtesy and concern for his comfort, but did so in perfect vernacular Kikuyu.

Thus the two began the long pantomime of ambiguity, allusion, suggestion, half-truth and half-lie that comprised the parable rich, idiomatic process of reaching an understanding in Kikuyu. Henderson walked away several hours later with a 40- page transcript of what had been said, and for the first time a clear and complete understanding of the military formations of Mount Kenya was available to British intelligence. Nothing had been

7 The policy of Villagisation in Kenya had been in the pipeline for some time, but was rubber-stamped in June of 1954 and rapidly put into effect in all of the key Kikuyu reserves. The concept involved the forced resettlement of the passive population into organised and protected villages. Ostensibly the objective was to shelter them from guerrilla attacks, but in reality the primary motivation was to isolate guerrilla units from their traditional support bases and to deny them access to food and, perhaps more importantly, intelligence. Claims that the programme, which without doubt added to the burden of an already distressed population, was aimed in part to punish Mau Mau sympathisers within the general population have probably been overstated. The tactic was part of an overall effort to further strangulate and isolate Mau Mau forest gangs. It was estimated that by early 1955 over one million Kikuyu had been resettled in protected villages. [*Maloba* p. 90]

Suspects rounded up for interrogation.

revealed that could directly harm those still active; China had been cautious to a fault in this regard, but a great deal in general terms had emerged, to draw into much sharper focus the official picture of Mau Mau.

Much of what China had revealed in his lengthy interview with Henderson was in fact easily corroborated thanks to the capture shortly afterwards of a key member of his operational company who had in his possession a cache of documents detailing the organisation and supply of all the Mount Kenya forces. In combination this was undoubtedly the most significant intelligence coup so far achieved by Special Branch, which of course would have added a great deal of momentum to the overall military/police preparations underway to take on Mau Mau in their home bases.

In the meanwhile, China did indeed face trial, as he had expected, and thanks in part to the absolute candour of his earlier interview with Henderson, and no doubt his general sense of pride in his achievements, his defence strategy was rather hopeless, and he was found guilty of consorting with terrorists and sentenced to hang. This, however, would not be the end of the story.

Waruhiu Itote emerges from his own and other biographical accounts as a tough and ruthless political enforcer and guerrilla leader, but also as a genial, amusing and charismatic man. His journey to prominence in the movement followed a reasonably well-travelled route. He was born in 1922 to a family of prosperous and politically alert landholders in the Mukurwe-ini division, Nyeri District, receiving little formal education thanks to his father's general aversion of the European system, but eventually finding himself in a King's African Rifles Signal Corps on active service in Burma. In 1946 he was demobilised, returning to Kenya to much fanfare but limited prospects, after which he was easily absorbed into Nairobi's Forty Group, joining other military veterans as the seeds of Mau Mau were beginning to germinate.[8] Later he became a strong-arm member of the *Muhimu*, serving as an oath administrator, enforcer and executioner.

In August 1952 China took to the forests of Mount Kenya ahead of a police crackdown on *Muhimu* activity in the Nyeri District. His capture in January 1954, after some 16 months of active campaigning, coincided more or less with the point at which the fortunes of Mau Mau had begun to turn, but also with other factors beginning to take shape on the wider stage

[8] The Forty Group was an early Kenyan criminal/social/political organisation of the mid-20th century comprising mainly members of the Kenya African Union who joined with the aim of using violence to make their message heard. The name is a translation of the Kikuyu phrase *Anake a 40*, which means 'The Young Men of 40'. The number 40 is a reference to the year 1940, in which most of the group's core members were drafted into the British Armed Forces.

Captured Mau Mau.

A British Army Bren gun team.

that might have suggested to him that the fight had already been superseded. By June of that same year Gold Coast nationalist leader Kwame Nkrumah would stand at the head of an interim government in Accra that would lead within two years to full independence for Ghana. Nigeria similarly adopted a pre-independence constitution in 1954 and Sierra Leone likewise. Discussion in Whitehall had already begun to touch on the likelihood of some similar constitutional accommodation to Black Nationalism in Kenya, making a virtue out a necessity one might suppose. Indeed, in February 1954, just a month after General China's capture, the Colonial Secretary, Oliver Lyttelton, arrived in Nairobi carrying with him in his briefcase plans for just such a new constitution.

Therefore, when, as China languished on death row in Nairobi and was approached there by his erstwhile interrogator Ian Henderson with a bold plan to initiate surrender negotiations with the hard core of the movement, he was immediately sympathetic to the idea. He certainly was a lot better informed after a few months on the outside than his colleagues on Mount Kenya, and he could probably see that for all intents and purposes the armed insurrection had run its course. Kenyan independence had been placed on the wider political agenda, a fact that was beyond the power of any beleaguered white settler community to influence, so all that remained was to negotiate a safe return for the forest fighters and thereafter to leave the political transition to the politicians.

The operation to bring the fighters in was codenamed *Wedgewood*, for the obvious name association, and in simple terms it required China to reach back through a series of planted letters to his fellow commanders with an invitation to negotiate a surrender. The planning was undertaken in the utmost secrecy because Baring, having already been flogged a number of times by the settler backlash, was understandably very nervous of a possible reaction from the Highlands. Erskine too braced himself for a likely storm when word eventually seeped out. China, in the meanwhile, was quietly granted a judicial pardon, which in the first instance startled the settler community, but did not alert it, after which Erskine agreed to suspend the work of Operation *Anvil* in order to facilitate the safe movement of enemy combatants out of the forest and through the reserves. Thereafter, General China, in the company of Ian Henderson, flew to Nyeri to establish a Special Branch operating headquarters to facilitate the operation.[9]

If handled sensitively and with patience the operation held out very reasonable chances of success. It needs to be borne in mind, however, that by then organisation in the forests was crumbling and the mood of the majority altered. Operation *Anvil* had effectively quarantined Mount Kenya and the Aberdares while throughout the Prohibited Areas tracks had been cut deep into the forests in order to more easily move in large numbers of troops. In addition, miles of fortified trenches had been dug to ring in the forest perimeter, attended to at intervals by armed Home Guard or Kenya Police posts.[10] The rebellion was effectively over, and the rebels on the run. Even if they had been able in any meaningful way to penetrate into the reserves, their chance of finding help or succour there was by then almost nil. They were now hunted, haunted, hungry, suspicious and alert. Although a great many guerrillas – and it was estimated then that less than 2,000 were still at large – would willingly have abandoned the movement if it could be guaranteed that they would not hang. There were others, of course, in particular those originals at the higher command level, who were considerably more circumspect about surrender

---

[9] Henderson was deeply involved in the operation, although direct negotiations were handled by government officials. Henderson was awarded the George Medal for his contribution, his citation reading in part: "Between February 13 and April 10, 1954. Mr Henderson was in immediate command of the Special Branch detachment assigned the duty of attempting to bring about a meeting between Government representatives, and those of the terrorists in the Mount Kenya area. The nature of the assignment made it necessary for Mr Henderson to travel frequently into the forests and parts of the reserve occupied by terrorists under conditions of extreme vulnerability in order to achieve this objective'.

[10] ... eighteen feet wide and ten feet deep, the most primeval of military obstacles, the *fosse*. Along its bed bristled thousands of sharpened stakes and these were augmented by miles of barbed wire which had been booby trapped. At half-mile intervals there were police posts and the half-mile between them was continuously patrolled by night and by day. Massed African labour created this ditch and it proved a highly successful barrier to the barefoot Mau Mau terrorist.

and still to some extent committed to the armed struggle.

The spoiler once again, however, was Dedan Kimathi. Here again we have a Nyeri man who took to the forests ahead of police pressure in late 1952, and who rose thereafter to what ought to have been a high command, but which was, as we have heard, always somewhat less than that. He was a darker character than China, who was both an honest thug and a cunning tactician, making no pretences to be otherwise. Kimathi, on the other hand, tended to cultivate about himself an aura of mysticism. He dabbled in a cult of personality, and indeed, very early on in the game seemed to lose his grip on his own paranoia, which, in the company of some degree of psychosis, resulted in periodic bouts of fratricidal bloodletting. These in fact caused one later Mau Mau capture to remark to his British handlers: "Nobody has helped the government as much as Kimathi, and for that reason he should be given a salary. He has killed more Mau Mau than any member of the Security Forces."[28]

Whatever might have been Kimathi's emotional failures, and the general state of his mind, he was acutely alert to the ebb and flow of matters, and was naturally keenly interested when news began to circulate that a surrender offer was on the table. He immediately called a meeting of all the high-ranking forest leaders of the Aberdares where it was established that a general consensus in favour of negotiations existed. A message was returned to the effect that a delegation would be sent to meet with the government. Unfortunately, that message did not reach the Special Branch operations desk, and was as a consequence not acknowledged. This led Kimathi to suppose that his particular overtures were being ignored – he learned soon afterwards that another high-ranking general, General Tanganyika, had turned himself over to the British in order to participate in the surrender. Soon afterwards, Tanganyika returned to the forest with a second series of letters addressed to the Mount Kenya commanders.

Kimathi seized on the perceived slight of being excluded from what he suspected might be a unilateral surrender on the part of the Mount Kenya forces. He thus began to apply his considerable energy and power of persuasion to discredit the process and undermine support for it among his key confederates in the Aberdares.

There were other difficulties too. Baring, fearful of news leaking, and claims against him of duplicity being made to add to everything else, made a public announcement coming clean with regards to what had been underway by then for some weeks. The response in Nairobi, and in certain key committee areas in and around the White Highlands, was predictable enough, although most harmful perhaps was the immediate unofficial refusal to cooperate on the part of district level police and officials, an attitude that resulted in administrative obstructions at every turn and a great deal of difficulty in expediting the process safely and effectively.

Then a highly regrettable incident took place that threw the entire operation into confusion, and ultimately killed it. Thanks to Kimathi, no specific line of communication existed between Special Branch and the Aberdare Forest, but, although tenuous and imperilled at times, communications with Mount Kenya remained open, and in fact had been strengthened towards the end of March 1954 by the defection of another powerful Mount Kenya commander, General Kaleba. From this point, cautious but substantive discussions began to take place between various official representatives – Generals China, Kaleba, Tanganika and five others, with Henderson always in attendance – and an eventual draft understanding was reached on the matter of amnesties and other terms of surrender. It was agreed thereafter that in order for those wishing to surrender to be able to marshall safely on the edge of the forest, a ceasefire would be respected within certain specified areas.

The negotiators duly returned to the Mount Kenya forest with the terms of surrender in hand. Furious divisions were then provoked among the various groups and individuals, and it took a long time, and a great deal of emotional and divisive debate, before any kind of consensus could be reached. From his seat in the Aberdares, Kimathi campaigned vociferously against any kind of surrender; with the eventual understanding reached that no understanding existed at all. Individuals were afforded the right to do what they would, and the matter left thus.

On 6 April 1954 some 1,000 Mount Kenya fighters were assembled and camped in readiness to surrender, waiting for another 600 to join them. They were identified by a KAR patrol positioned just within the boundary of the reserve. The guerrillas were aware of the presence of the KAR but did not feel threatened under the common understanding of the ceasefire rules. There has been some discrepancy unearthed regarding precisely where the guerrillas were located in regards to ceasefire boundaries, and this might have been so, but all army units would certainly have been aware of what was afoot and were well within their discretionary rights to avoid hostile action. However, in the mood of the times, this did not happen. The following day the KAR launched an attack, killing 25 guerrillas and capturing seven more.

It is hard to imagine anything more deleterious to the building of trust under such circumstances than this. The local brigade commander, Brigadier Reginald Orr, pointed to the technicalities and pronounced himself fully at ease with the consequences of his orders. General Erskine was almost beside himself with frustration, but seeing things for what they were, and recognising the procedural correctness of what had taken place, offered no reprimands and put the whole matter down to bad luck. General China's reputation was shattered – he was sent north to serve out the Emergency in the company of Jomo Kenyatta – while Kimathi was thoroughly vindicated. And with the stealthy approach now hopelessly compromised, the emphasis returned to war. There were by this point very few fighters left at large anyway, and what was in effect left to do was simply mopping up. Henderson, however, now fixed his sights on Kimathi. The rules of engagement had narrowed significantly. This was cat-and-mouse as never before, and although hardly war on a massive scale, the final acts of Mau Mau in the end turned out to be, militarily at least, the most interesting and instructive phase of the conflict.

CHAPTER FIVE:

THE LONG GOODBYE

"For months the sole preoccupation of all of these terrorists had been mere survival. They lived like animals. They survived because of their animal skills, and when caught they reacted like animals"

—*Ian Henderson*

The long tedium of the Operation *Anvil* interrogations came to an end in mid-1954, some four months after the launch of the operation. The initial detentions had been fairly promptly expedited, but thereafter the exhaustive process of minutely screening the 70,000 or so Kikuyu males isolated from the general black population of Nairobi went on. Those identified as suspect were removed to specially prepared detention camps while family members were collected and removed to the reserves. The intelligence haul was, of course, extensive, and took within itself several months to collate and analyse. Special Branch now understood in fine detail the inner workings of Mau Mau, and systematically moved to disrupt it. Along with those identified in Operation *Anvil* were those implicated during interrogation. A steady stream of urban and rural passive wing members were rounded up in ongoing follow-up raids known as *Pepper Pots*, conducted by special intelligence teams that kept the Mau Mau system off-balance, inhibiting any meaningful revival.

Thereafter, General Erskine was able to concentrate his energy on a number of secondary factors. One of these was chronic command and control deficits that existed at the highest level of the colonial system. At the onset of violence, security-related operations had been coordinated by an improvised body known as the SITREP (situation report) Committee, comprising administration, police and military officials, but with neither possessing the authority nor general efficiency to undertake a military-style campaign. This body was replaced in 1953 by the Colony Emergency Committee, which was typically chaired by the Governor, and included his deputy and representatives of the General Officer Commanding, the Chief Secretary and the members for Finance, Agriculture and African Affairs.

Present also at the fortnightly meetings would usually be the fractious and vocal leader of the settler community, Michael Blundell, who could be relied upon on most occasions to try the patience of General Erskine and further fray the nerves of the Governor. Subordinate to this committee was a second called the Deputy Director of Operations Committee, presided over by General Hinde, who served under Erskine as Deputy Director of Operations, and under whose direction policy initiated by the Colony Emergency Committee was acted upon, and material for policy decisions submitted.

Erskine, who had no small amount of command experience behind him, found this unwieldy process deeply frustrating, and moved quickly upon his arrival in the colony to rationalise

A captured Mau Mau weapon, which appears to be a modified Lee Enfield.

Kenyan police arresting two Mau Mau terrorists in a village.

it. Taking advantage of a direct line of communications with the Colonial Secretary, who tended to share his low opinion of matters on the ground in Kenya, Erskine was able to introduce a simpler and more streamlined War Council that included himself, Baring, Deputy Governor Sir Frederick Crawford and the ubiquitous Michael Blundell. This group met twice weekly, referring to a dedicated secretariat in order to ensure that motions passed were acted upon promptly and effectively.

Thus, as 1955 dawned, not only was the Mau Mau manifestly on the run, but Erskine had accumulated sufficient manpower and matériel to saturate the Prohibited Areas, and had, moreover, given himself the necessary framework of authority to achieve a final solution. By December 1954, intelligence estimates suggested that Mau Mau numbers had dwindled to under 4,000. Increasingly competent and aggressive army patrols had had the effect over the preceding months of keeping active Mau Mau gangs mobile and unsettled, allowing them neither easy access into the reserves or commercial farming areas for the purpose of resupply, nor any opportunity to settle long enough in the forest to forage, lay snares or cultivate. Expeditions beyond the immediate safety of the forest had now become perilously dangerous, causing famished gangs to steal what they could when they could, with the result that sympathetic villagers were often pillaged regardless of their affinities, eroding popular support even further, and even more completely isolating active units within their mountain redoubts.

It ought to be remembered that the highland reaches of Mount Kenya and the Aberdares Range were then, and remain today, although slightly less so, characterised by several distinct ecological zones. From approximately 6,500ft upwards the mountains are ringed by montane forest to varying degrees of density, depending on the concentrations of population and the extent of land utilisation. Above this, in a belt tending to be more concentrated on the east-facing slopes, corresponding with the zones of highest rainfall, lies the bamboo belt, a uniquely challenging environment of close-packed bamboo emerging from many layers of broken detritus and mulch through which any kind of movement, notwithstanding at a very steep gradient, was extremely difficult. Beyond this lay a thinner but somewhat steeper belt of woodland or forest, before the timberline gave way entirely to open moorland punctuated by ooze zones and vast areas of moss-covered bogs and rocky outcrops. Finally, the upper reaches of the mountain tended to be high desert with rarefied atmospheres and bitter cold.

Thus it can fairly easily be imagined how life for Mau Mau in the forests had devolved into a bitter fight for survival against the elements, hampered by relentless military pressure and increasing internal infighting and distrust. The evolution of pseudo gangs, of which more will be heard later, made it almost impossible for gangs or individuals not known to one another to interact and cooperate without the fear that one or the other might be working on the government side.

The large camp clusters and operational groups that had characterised Mau Mau during 1953 and the early months of 1954 had by the beginning of 1955 been broken up and scattered. Most moved first into the bamboo zone, and then higher into the timberline forest, finding it ever more difficult to maintain an existence where very little game flourished and where physical conditions were extremely harsh. This being the state of play by January 1955, General Erskine launched Operation *Hammer. Hammer* was conceived initially as a massive sweep of the extensive Aberdare moorlands in division strength with a view to driving Mau Mau groups back down into the forest and into the waiting arms of prepositioned ambushes and stops. A similar operation codenamed Operation *First Flute* hoped to achieve the same result on Mount Kenya.

Neither operation, considering the relative weight of manpower and ordnance brought to bear, achieved much. Those surviving Mau Mau combatants simply melted back into the forest, manifestly failing to reappear in the many security force ambushes and stops that ringed the mountain. By then the extraordinary bushcraft of the average Mau Mau had transmogrified among those surviving hardcore into something almost mythic. Casualty rates for the operation were minimal – some 150 killed or captured on the Aberdares – leading to the statistic that running to ground a single Mau Mau fighter cost a conservative average of £10,000.

British troops on a 'stop and search' patrol.

Peter Hewitt by one of the gorges on the Kinangop plateau, which appears deceptively shallow. Mau Mau gangs foraging for food might elude security force patrols for weeks ensconced in the densely vegetated bowels of such gorges. Sweeps along the roaring rivers below were both arduous and slow.
Photo Peter Hewitt

The idea of broad and comprehensive sweeping strategy devolved quickly into the somewhat simpler and more sophisticated tactic of Domination of Areas, in which army units would be given defined areas of moorland and forest to occupy and dominate. Here they could be expected to develop a general familiarity and an operating procedure that would make it difficult for any guerrilla groups to move in and take refuge. This system worked much better, and yielded 277 killed or captured on Mount Kenya within a few weeks of implementation.

As this was underway a second surrender offer was made in response to tentative overtures towards a general ceasefire extended by insurgent leaders, including, very briefly, Dedan Kimathi. Kimathi, however, changed his mind as he was apt to do, doing his best to influence others. This resulted in a second failed attempt at a negotiated surrender, although during this period some 1,000 fighters did surrender by their own initiative. These on the whole represented what was regarded as the defensive outer ring of key guerrilla leaders, which, of course, very quickly opened up renewed channels of offensive penetration for the increasingly energised pseudo gangs. Erskine and Baring, needless to say, once against absorbed furious accusations of cowardice and betrayal from the increasingly confident settler committees.

The timing of this latest amnesty offer is interesting. The Kikuyu Guard, at one time arguably the main weapon used to break the back of Mau Mau, had since then developed into something of an offensive movement in its own right, with official command and control tending to have less and less influence upon it. The organisation, alongside other loyalist groups, controlled the reserves with an iron fist, maintaining a hostile posture towards Mau Mau and attacking it at every opportunity, but also devolving somewhat into an enforcement agency dealing more often with localised enemies and subsisting increasingly on corruption and racketeering. The upside of this was that open support of Mau Mau was now virtually impossible, but the downside was the official fear that if not disarmed and brought quickly under control a mass desertion might take place which would introduce a potentially disastrous third force into the conflict, a prospect about which Erskine for one was a great deal less than sanguine. Commissioner of Police O'Rourke, upon his retirement in May 1954, aired his misgivings about the Kikuyu Guard, predicting that the freedom to act that they had been given would soon produce complications that might not easily be contained: "The sooner, therefore, it [the Home Guard] can be disarmed," O'Rourke wrote in a private dispatch to Sir Hugh Fraser, at that time Parliamentary Private Secretary to Oliver Lyttelton, "... dispensed with and its strongholds removed after the main threat of Mau Mau violence is dealt with, the sooner can there be law and order enforced in Kikuyu country."

Attempting to diminish the strength and tighten discipline within the ranks of the Kikuyu Guard, however, while at the same time offering what remained of the active Mau Mau an amnesty, was quite obviously an extremely risky and delicate strategy.[11] Needless to say, upon the news becoming general, rural committees in all the settled districts met in animated sessions, with one, that of Tigoni in the Kiambu District, being particularly vocal. A right-wing action group known as the Tigoni Tigers demanded the resignation of the War Council for "this and their past pathetic performance". Special emergency legislation was elsewhere required to prevent white extremists issuing leaflets that, by threat, attempted to discourage those among the insurgents who might wish to surrender.[29]

In May 1955, Erskine at least was able to kiss it all goodbye.. It was then that his term of service expired and he handed over command to his successor, General Sir Gerald Lathbury. Erskine left the territory with a minimum of regret, but also not without the satisfaction of knowing that the job had been well done. Mau Mau had, for all intents and purposes, been defeated.

[11] The offers made in January 1955 included an assurance that guerrillas who surrendered would not be prosecuted for any terrorist offences, even those that were liable for the death penalty, although they would be detained for a given period. In the meanwhile, members of the Kikuyu Guard were told of a forthcoming reorganisation and assured that no action would be taken in respect of the past but strict discipline would be required for the future.

CHAPTER SIX:

SPECIAL FORCES

Lathbury inherited a very different situation to that which Erskine had taken on two years earlier. This, however, tended to suit somewhat the differing natures of the two men. Despite considerable battlefield experience, Erskine had always had about him the flavour of a staff officer rather than a fighting general. His introduction into the army had been through the King's Royal Rifle Corps, with which he had served during the First World War in France and Belgium, so it could hardly be said of him that he lacked exposure. However, by the time the Second World War broke he was a senior staff officer, returning to the field in North Africa, perhaps a little reluctantly, and from there following the war more or less to its conclusion in various operational commands. In Europe, however, he suffered some criticism for over-caution, and was replaced as commander of the 7th Armoured Division during the crucial last few months, concluding his service in an arguably more productive role as head of the Supreme Headquarters Allied Expeditionary Force Mission to Belgium, and then General Officer Commanding the 43rd Wessex Division.

In the post-war period Erskine's career tended towards senior military command positions in such places as Hong Kong, Egypt and, of course, Kenya. Kenya, however, he regarded as something that he would rather not have had to deal with, his objective by then being to plot an easy course towards retirement, which, incidentally, he found to be wholly satisfactory, serving until his death in 1965 in the very respectable role of Aide-de-Camp General to Her Majesty the Queen.

Lathbury, on the other hand, was nothing less than a fighting soldier. He inherited a clear military mindset from his father, Colonel (Henry) Oscar Lathbury, which was no doubt polished to a high gloss at Sandhurst from where he was commissioned in 1926 into the Oxfordshire and Buckinghamshire Light Infantry. In 1936 he served for four years on secondment to the Royal West

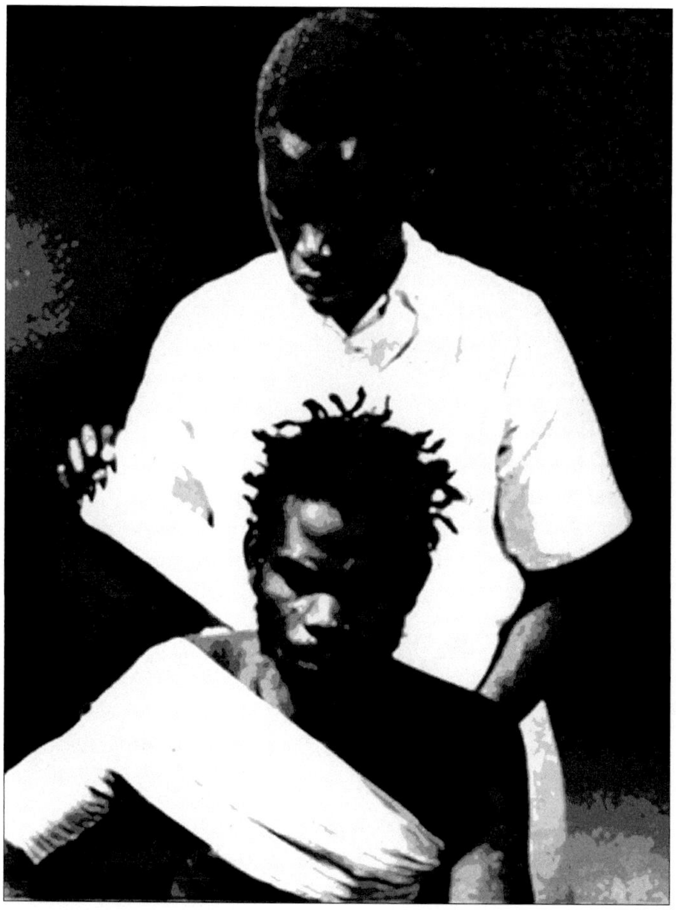

A wounded Mau Mau capture.

A King's African Rifles soldier poses with a comrade from the Black Watch.

African Frontier Force and Gold Coast Regiment. This was more of Africa than Erskine had ever seen, orbiting, as he had, the North African and Mediterranean theatres; moreover Lathbury understood more acutely the practicalities of dealing with native troops, and was no less familiar with southern and east African colonials. It was these men who, quite often, served on short-term detachments commanding platoons, companies and battalions of West African troops, particularly during the East African and Burma campaigns of the Second World War, and from whom lessons in the peculiarities of African soldiering could be learned.

Lathbury saw considerable combat during the Second World War, and in fact raised and commanded airborne and parachute brigades that took part in Operation *Market Garden*, with he as Officer Commanding. He was portrayed in the film *A Bridge Too Far* by Scottish actor Donald Douglas, which in fact rather understated Lathbury's battlefield achievements. He was later wounded and briefly captured, serving in Holland as a prisoner of war before escaping and eventually linking up again with Allied forces.

His post-war career was something of a mixed bag of military administrative and command roles, as well as secondments to the Imperial Defence College and the War Office as Director General of Military Training. He also, incidentally, took part in the Harold Hall Australian Expeditions on behalf of the British Museum of Natural History to help complete the general antipodean ornithological list.

All of this tends to paint a picture of a rugged but cerebral soldier whose understanding of an unconventional battlefield could be relied upon to be more focused than his predecessor. Erskine, however, had had neither the interest nor the opportunity to ponder the finer arts of counter-insurgency, but rather the broader framework of command and control, and a certain amount of political diplomacy in a very difficult environment. He had anyway effectively won the war by simply recognising the signature weakness of Mau Mau, and crushing its command and logistics capacity with one heavy and well-aimed blow. Thereafter, the question simply became one of how to bring the whole affair to a quick and satisfactory conclusion. The business of how to deal with a militarily ineffectual force of diehard guerrillas deep in a tropical forest could be left to a man with the creativity to do it. This was the work of special forces, so let a special forces commander handle it.

Lathbury made a quick appraisal of the situation and concluded that the use of military assets in large-scale ground coverage and sweep operations had outlived its usefulness. Mau Mau now consisted of a rag tag coalescence of fugitives preoccupied primarily with individual survival, motivated in the main by a fear of the consequences of surrender and with the hard core of leadership, such as it still remained, largely determined to fight to the death.

The remaining 2,000 or so fighters at large quite obviously had ceased to represent any kind of military or security threat, but their continued existence remained a focal point for violent resistance and lawlessness, and moreover represented a symbolically important deferment of absolute defeat. Soon afterwards, therefore, Lathbury authorised the withdrawal of

A pseudo team. The two men, left and centre, are 'turned' terrorists, while the one on the right is a white man.

Internees awaiting security processing.

the main military force from the forest, transferring two British battalions out of the territory and allowing a KAR battalion to return to its base in Uganda. In the meanwhile he had made it his business to familiarise himself with the situation on the ground, and was extremely impressed with what he heard about the local special operations teams that had, for over a year, been developing the concept of pseudo gangs in order to locate and either destroy or bring in the isolated gangs and small groups that were still roaming fugitive in the forests.

It is here that we touch on a very interesting aspect of the story of Mau Mau, interesting on the one hand for the tactical innovation that it represented, but interesting also because of the enduring iconography that grew out of it: white special forces men merging with black turned guerrillas, and entering the dark and primal forest to match wits with the elusive Micks. Likewise, it was the period, after several years of life in the forest, that the popular image of the Mau Mau fighter emerged.

Prior to Operation *Anvil*, the forest fighters had lived reasonably well. In the aftermath of *Anvil*, however, the situation altered very much for the worse. As the security force and the Home Guard cordon tightened around the Prohibited Areas the larger Mau Mau gangs quickly began to be squeezed very hard. Then, later, as the military tracks began to cut into the forest and the army began to cover ground more comprehensively, survival in the mountains became very difficult. Large groups were forced to fragment while operational capacity almost evaporated, with only very random and dispersed attacks taking place for little purpose other than the theft or seizure of foodstuffs. From this the typical portrait of a Mau Mau fighter emerged as an odd amalgam of Cubanesque revolutionary icon and vermin-infested, locust-eating zealot. Their almost superhuman special awareness had come about simply as a by-product of a very deep plunge back into the practicalities of stone age life; and perhaps too the result of a great deal of attrition and the associated natural selection that would logically occur.

A Mau Mau operative who had been in the forest for several years would usually be characterised by peculiarities of dress, appearance and smell. Surviving in the damp, cathedral-like recesses of the highland forests of Kenya would very quickly decay the clothing that was originally brought into the forest, and once the art of repair had completely been exhausted, most fighters would begin to adopt homemade garments and accessories made from animal skins and other natural products. These began as a matter of necessity, but in actual fact soon developed into a uniform of sorts, that, depending on the animal skin used, would define rank and importance. Blue or Sykes monkey skins were commonly used, thanks to both the availability of these creatures and the highly adapted camouflage that they offered. Red bushbuck was another commonly used skin type, tree hyrax another, with such lush creatures as leopard yielding their pelts only for high-ranking members. Very little if any footwear was ever utilised, which was not unusual at the time, and in fact the convention of barefoot *askari* had only given way to proper regimental footwear for native troops during the First World War. It was a source of frequent wonder to whites the extent to which a black man's feet could develop a layer of horn on the sole that defeated any boot in critical circumstances and, although hardly attractive, was always extremely functional.

The matted braids that grew after years of sartorial neglect occasioned by life in the forest also came to characterise Mau Mau, but in fact were cultivated for the practical purpose of easy lice removal under circumstances where washing and personal hygiene had long ago been abandoned. This, within itself, tended to create the last characteristic that most whites noticed first when encountering an active Mau Mau fighter: his smell. The combination of years of not washing, of hide clothing that was rarely if ever removed, along with regular saturation by sweat, urine and faeces, as well as the blood of snared wild animals or slaughtered livestock, produced a stench that has been variously described by many authors, each conceding in the end the inadequacy of any written language to do justice to the phenomenon. Lastly, it was the primal, animalistic attitude of recently captured Mau Mau that caught the attention of their captors: the furtive movement, the fidgeting restlessness and extreme skittishness and alertness to threat, noticeable most commonly in a man's eyes that could never rest for long on a single subject. This was the moral characteristic of men who had been submerged for so long in deeply primitive conditions, relying on nothing but their wits and acumen for basic survival, and who had learned by this to interpret the slightest signals of nature and man to alert them to safety or danger.

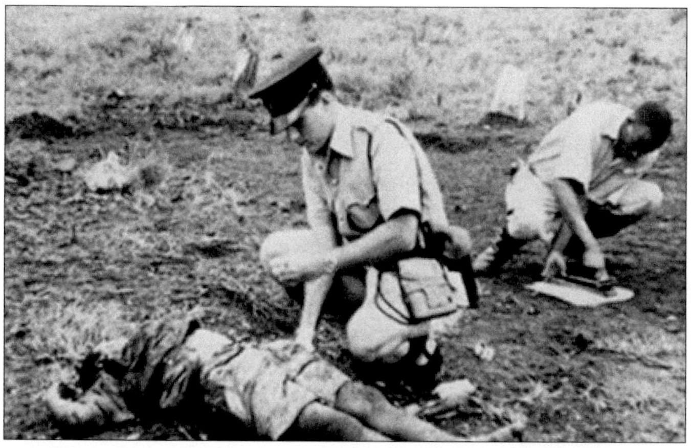

A white policeman fingerprints a dead Mau Mau killed during an attack on a police post.

Black Nairobi citizens are stopped and searched by British troops.

These were the hold-outs, the men for whom survival and bushcraft had been cultivated to the finest manifestation possible, making them extremely difficult to pin down by conventional means, and very difficult to catch under any circumstances; capturing now being key, since, as Peter Hewitt put it, fresh intelligence was always worth much more than another dead Mau Mau.

To capture a guerrilla required another guerrilla, at the very least, and the Mau Mau subverted to this purpose needed to be handled by a very particular breed of white man. These were the white pseudo operators, men who have tended to be over immortalised in the literature of such writers as Robert Ruark and Ian Henderson, and have as a consequence become no less part of the Mau Mau mythology than the woolly-haired Mick himself. And although neither stereotype really reflects the whole truth, both nonetheless have a story behind them.

The use of Kikuyu trackers and interpreters had been an obvious first step in getting to know the battlefield. The practice had first been adopted by rural white police details patrolling alongside their black constables, which led relatively quickly and easily toward the practice of disguising loyal Kikuyu as Mau Mau and allowing them to enter the forest in order to make contact with authentic guerrilla gangs. These groups were, in actual fact, quite rarely accompanied by a white security detail, blacked-up to impersonate a guerrilla.

The rarity of this possibly had much to do with the fact that very few white men capable of such a ruse existed, and possibly too because the myth of a white man being able to successfully impersonate a black man in order to deceive a group of individuals as perceptively acute as Mau Mau was precisely that, a myth. It was possible for a white man to be part of a pseudo group so long as he kept quiet and kept to the background, and when it did happen, this tended to be the procedure. However, it made more sense, and was certainly safer, for pseudo groups to be made up entirely of turned Mau Mau and operating with a Special Branch or Field Intelligence Assistant (FIA) handler not directly involved in any covert operations.

For the most part the objective of these operations was to gather intelligence rather than to actively engage the enemy. Any offensive action that might result from intelligence gathered in this way usually took place once the pseudo gang had left the area. This was obviously in order to avoid active Mau Mau putting two and two together and concluding that a programme of warfare by other means was underway, and also to avoid compromising pseudo groups in order that they could continue operating.

Frank Kitson, a British Military Intelligence officer, of whom we have already heard, is quite often credited with the birth of the concept of pseudo operations in Kenya, although in truth it was simply he who saw the wider potential of a very informal practice and set about organising it and placing it on a proper military footing. In trying to achieve this, and in trying to convince many others higher up the command ladder that this was a worthwhile idea, he fought an uphill battle. It is a widely appreciated fact that military innovation more often than not occurs from the ground up, and had it not been for Lathbury, who was quite the kind of soldier to see the value of unconventional approaches to an unorthodox military problem, the use of pseudo operators might very well have remained a low key and selectively applied tactic.

Kitson's early efforts as one of the first District Military Intelligence Officers seconded from the army had been to attempt, in the aftermath of the Lari Massacre and other high-profile Mau Mau operations, to flesh out the overall intelligence picture with a view to informing operation planning and decision-making. With a far better grasp of general organisational efficiency than the peculiarities of the Kikuyu, which was probably under the circumstances of more practical use to him, he was fairly quickly able to reflect with satisfaction that his organisation was beginning to make a real contribution towards the general increase in operational successes. He was, however, concerned that much of the information gained and disseminated through official channels tended to be rather non-specific, with little that could be gleaned for a security force commander to frame offensive operations.

According to Kitson:

> However energetically we might rush about the District, and however much we could pick up, we could only get what the Mau Mau gave us accidentally, such as information gained from observation or from interrogating prisoners. Even our interrogation was inefficient because it is very difficult to make any sense out of prisoners' stories unless you know

> something to start with. A little advance information enables the interrogator to trip up his prisoner when the lying starts.[30]

Having achieved a broad intelligence framework Kitson then began to give thought to how best to gain the sort of operational intelligence that would put local emergency committees more fully in the picture with regards to what was pending rather than what had already happened. Initially Kitson's thought process tended to be focused on the rather orthodox idea of positioning camps in each division wherein groups of loyal Kikuyu could be based in order to assist with interrogations and to cultivate a local networks of informers. The development of this initial structure advanced matters somewhat, but it still lacked any kind of official endorsement, and was undertaken in an *ad hoc* manner and without a specific budget.

At the end of March 1954, meanwhile, an apparently insignificant discovery proved to be pivotal in the identification of the elusive key to accurate and up-to-date operational intelligence. The killing of a guerrilla during a small action in the Gatundu area produced a notebook that it was assumed belonged to some sort of a clerk or scribe within a wider gang structure, and which, upon examination, yielded names of each guerrilla active within the district, the dates on which they had joined and the registered numbers of their weapons. Based on this Kitson was able to assemble a card index, adding to what was determined from the notebook supplementary intelligence gained from headmen in the home area of the gang. From this source it could reasonably accurately be determined where, within the reserve, that the gang was finding assistance, and from where they would be most likely to look for access to supplies and information. This did not, in and of itself, offer much that would assist security forces in contacting the gang, but it did provide an extremely accurate profile of each member, which, in the event that one of these was captured, would facilitate somewhat the extraction of more reliable intelligence.

And this, indeed, is precisely what happened. A few

A captured Mau Mau, wounded in a firefight, is brought into the compound of Gilgil police station. *Photo Peter Hewitt*

Peter Hewitt (far right) with members of his Tracker Combat Team and the Gloucestershire Regiment, having successfully contacted a large terrorist gang on Mountt Kipipiri. The patrol was guided to the enemy hideout by a 'turned' Mau Mau surrenderee (third from left). *Photo Peter Hewitt*

weeks later a prisoner, identified as James, was brought in by the Home Guard. Kitson decided to conduct the interrogation himself. Confronted with the usual feigned ignorance and fervent denials, he decided to confront his prisoner with the contents of the 'book'. Addressing a black clerk through the open door of the interrogation room, who happened to be outside of the field of vision of the prisoner and upon whose desk the book lay, Kitson clicked his fingers, raised his hands and called out "Book!", whereupon the clerk tossed the book through the doorway and into Kitson's upheld hand. James, who had not seen the clerk, was astonished. To him it appeared that his interrogator had simply summoned the book with a snap of his fingers, at which command it had arrived in his hand from the pocket of the gang clerk still deep in the forest, a level of magic that James had never before beheld, and no doubt could hardly resist. Thus, upon the assumption that all was known anyway, he opened a spigot of fresh intelligence that Kitson, over the course of several hours, eagerly recorded:

> At the end of that time we had a very accurate picture of both the Gatundu gang and the gang in the north of Thika because James had acted as a liaison officer between them. We also had James whose only wish was to stay with us and work against his former friends. We were more powerful than they were and only too pleased to accommodate him in his wish.[31]

Here Kitson was pleasantly surprised, as others had been, and would be again, at the willingness of captured guerrillas to work against their erstwhile comrades. At a later point the matter of 'turning' guerrillas would become a somewhat formularised process, playing on key weakness in the captured combatant's situation and grooming him by the use of a series of unexpected responses. In the beginning this behaviour was put down as just another Kuke foible: that being one of highly elastic standards of personal loyalty. Whites espousing this not altogether unpredictable theory tended to point to the Ruck murders, and the fact that an ostensibly devoted employee, with a proven record of loyalty, had been the willing catalyst to the events that brought about the murder of the family. A Kuke would turn on a penny: one day he would be tucking your five-year old into bed and next he was cleaving your skull with a panga.

In fact, the matter was more prosaic than this. A large number of Mau Mau had entered the forest for reasons other than unquenchable zealotry, often under duress, and quite often retained in the ranks by the threat of hanging should they be caught. To then be captured, and no doubt very roughly conveyed at the hands of the Home Guard to a police station, would only reinforce that sense of what the future held. But then, to be treated with kindness and consideration, to meet other guerrillas with a similar story, and to receive assurances that cooperation with the authorities would reap immediate reward, it is hardly surprising that the decision was made, and made very quickly.

And so it was. Future pseudo handlers frequently remarked on the ease of turning Micks. Somewhat later, in Rhodesia, as the Selous Scouts was being formed, perhaps the best known pseudo regiment to have emerged from Africa, recruiters were also surprised to encounter very little difficulty in systematically turning captured guerrillas, with very few instances recorded of turned fighters afterwards attempting to return to the struggle.

James, in the meanwhile, was put to work pointing out likely ambush locations and identifying loyalists, and once or twice, upon his own recognisance, returning to the forest to meet up with other fighters who were not aware that he had been turned, and thereafter passing on fresh intelligence to the FIAs. It took the chance observation of James sharing guerrilla protocols with other black security force details – anecdotal information such as handshakes, recognition etiquette and slang – for Kitson to experience an epiphany. James was Mau Mau. He instinctively thought and acted Mau Mau. And what is more he had taught others to do the same. The potential in this was huge. The idea was then exhaustively discussed and refined somewhat, followed by a few experimental patrols that tended to confirm the potential, after which it became simply a matter of selling the concept to GHQ.

It so happened, however, that this was an idea whose time had come. No sooner had things begun to fall into place than Erskine launched Operation *Anvil*. From that moment on the focus of the emergency shifted to the forests, and it would be the men who had proven proficiency in this environment who would retrieve the baton of active operations. Initially, of course, Erskine fell back on tried and tested strategies. However, the orthodox infantry units that flooded the operational areas took from the forests only what could be selected by a very wide-toothed comb, leaving behind a persistent residue that would ultimately require a much sharper instrument than conventional infantry to dislodge.

This undeniable truth was quite adequately borne out by the last substantive military operation of the Emergency – Operation *Dante* – which took place during the latter weeks of July 1955. This was the first operation of its kind undertaken under Lathbury's command, and which no doubt drove home to him the point that set-piece operations utilising massive quantities of manpower and ordnance were a gargantuan waste of time and money.

Involved in Operation *Dante* were four British Army battalions provided by the King's African Rifles, the Gloucestershire Regiment, the King's Shropshire Light Infantry and the Royal Irish Fusiliers. The procedure was highly formal and configured along a very simple and established plan. Troops would penetrate the forest along a wide perimeter to a depth of approximately 1,000 yards, after which the RAF and various artillery and mortar emplacements would bombard the forest in an effort to drive the Mau Mau outward and into prepositioned ambushes.

Enemy numbers in the Kiambu and Lari forests at that time, however, were estimated to be less than 300, so once again the War Council was placing its reliance on saturating the forest with troops, and carpeting the uplands with explosives in the hope of at least running a few of them to ground. In the event, the operation proved to be something of a fiasco. The British troops involved had very limited experience, coupled with the fact that

KC21 Gloster mortarmen in action during Operation *Bullrush*. Mortars did not prove effective.

bombing and artillery barrages had proved themselves time and again to be ineffective. A handful of Mau Mau were killed or captured, but at the cost of several British friendly-fire casualties and the death of battalion commander Lieutenant-Colonel Rupert Brooke-Smith. Operation *Dante* marked the end of security force reliance on large-scale military operations in the forests, marking also the moment that pseudo operations, or special forces as the programme had been officially named, took over.

Operation *Dante*, however, could at least be credited with introducing a new and extremely effective concept of attrition officially termed population sweeps. This tactic involved the mobilisation of large numbers of local community members, ironically in most cases women, to cover significant areas of ground in order to flush out Mau Mau. Many of the latter were recorded as having been chopped up into unrecognisable pieces by probably those most able users of the ubiquitous panga or *simi* in native society: women. Bear in mind that traditionally women did most of the heavy work, and were certainly, in most cases, the physical equal of any man.

According to Fred Majdalany:

> On one occasion in Meru, the District Officer, with cooperation of the Chiefs and Headmen, assembled 70,000 villagers, mostly women, and lined them up at the edge of the forest. On his signal the great line surged forward, the villagers hacking and shouting their way through the dense undergrowth with pangas. In their gaily coloured dressed and headscarves these laughing woman may have been a happy group of harvesters anywhere. But the way they cut to small pieces any Mau Mau caught in their path was a reminder that this was still Africa.[32]

These population sweeps, as effective as they were, were interesting also because they gave an indication of the degree to which public opinion had swung against Mau Mau. The few active fighters left at large were now even more securely isolated within the forest while local people were given a free hand in helping themselves in the matter of throwing off what had by then become an extremely burdensome and odious security situation, in particular as the parallel civil programme of screening and detentions continued quite as Mau Mau was beginning to breathe its last.

Frank Kitson, meanwhile, left the colony soon after Operation *Dante*, later becoming involved in the Malayan Emergency, the Falklands War and operations in Northern Ireland. By then the systematic and day-to-day deployment of special forces had been removed from his remit anyway, after which he had been reduced to the position of an interested observer. His last key contribution had been over the official status of the programme, and in presenting it to Lathbury for consideration at a meeting held at GHQ in June 1955, a month before Operation *Dante*.

The policy debate during this key meeting involved the difficulty of deciding whether pseudo operations should be run by the Operations or Intelligence Branch of the Security Forces. Arguments in both cases were compelling: those advocating that intelligence, and Special Branch in particular, should remain at the helm of pseudo ops did so on the basis that pseudo teams required at the very least to be armed with diverse, accurate and up-to-the-minute intelligence in order to operate safely and effectively. This, incidentally, was Kitson's position. However, a number of senior Special Branch officers were keenly vociferous in arguing an operational takeover of Special Forces, citing caution at Special Branch being put in control of what was quickly emerging as an offensive weapon rather than an intelligence-gathering tool, as it had initially been conceived.

Another point that Kitson was very keen to emphasise was that, no matter what body ultimately gained operational control of Special Forces, it was of vital importance that teams, when formed, should remain within their own areas. He was also adamant that pseudo teams should be controlled at a District HQ level, and based firmly within the static organisation of known Field Intelligence Assistants, who, bearing in mind the detailed work that had been undertaken in the months and years prior to this, would be those most able to provide the type of detailed and relevant moment-by-moment information that was needed for pseudo operations to succeed.

Kitson also argued for retaining a pseudo group within a given area, under the handling of specific FIAs, and remaining focused on operations against a specific gang, or gangs, about which they would naturally build a deep familiarity and a sense of mission. This was as opposed to the standard military position that pseudo operations would be based at some central point, away from their home areas, and utilised as and when needed to suit any given operational plan.

This, Kitson felt, would be watering down the effectiveness of pseudo operations and somewhat defeating the object.

At the GHQ meeting held in Nairobi on 4 June 1955, chaired, incidentally, by General Lathbury for the first time, Kitson was unexpectedly overruled. The organisational structure of special forces would be centralised near Nyeri, not only for training, but also for deployment and operations. Teams would be summoned to a given area by a District Emergency Committee where they would operate before returning to base to await another call. This, in many respects, would have thrust pseudo teams blind into any given area, robbing them of the intimate familiarity of long-term operations in an area, and without the cutting edge of viable intelligence that it had been proved, and would be proved again, that pseudo operators could not effectively function without.

In the event the principal of pseudo operations, when it was systematically applied, continued to work well, perhaps thanks in part to the fact that the centralised and organised special forces were less organised than might be supposed, and that much of the work done by Special Forces, and indeed the Combat Tracker Teams that had evolved parallel to Kitson's pseudo programme, had a rough and ready feel and did not always follow the preordained maxims of an operation. Nonetheless, soon after the GHQ meeting a Special Forces HQ was established at Nyeri that came under the remit of the Commissioner of Police rather than the army. Five pseudo teams were duly assembled, each comprising ten ex-Mau Mau and commanded by selected white operators. Tracker combat units were a slightly different concept to special force pseudo teams, with the emphasis, as the name implies, tending to be on the use of turned guerrillas for tracking and follow up rather than the systematic hunt for elusive guerrilla bands. The best and most engaging accounts of the Combat Tracker Team principle can be found in the memoirs of Peter Hewitt, who tells it like it is in a chapter of his thoroughly engaging memoir called 'How to Eliminate Elusive Micks':

> If police or military came to possess a captured terrorist, or for that matter a surrenderee, he had to be used while he was still red-hot – before the stench of rotten meat and fat had faded from his rags; before civilised surroundings had sent the lice scampering from his body; before the wide, expressionless stare disappeared from his eyes; before he ceased looking and behaving as an animal. If he was not exploited immediately for operational purposes, then the chances of a gang being successfully stalked in the camps he'd last occupied would be thinner than those of winning the treble chance on the football pools.[33]

This was indeed precisely what Kitson had argued, and what men at the tactical end of the business of operations knew without needing to be told, and frequently acted upon with or without official clearance.

Hewitt describes how early in 1955 localised experiments began with what was called a Stock Theft Investigation Team, responding to a spiking of Mau Mau stock thefts that corresponded with general efforts to strangle the organisation through all the many containment devices described above. These units were divided

KC24 The Colony Operations Room at Nairobi Police HQ. *Photo Peter Hewitt*

into an active investigation element and a tracker-combat element. The obvious rationale was that, upon receiving a report of stock theft, those tasked with investigation would do so, while those tasked with follow-up would immediately set off, disregarding the scene of the crime in order to follow what were usually fairly readable tracks left behind by animals. If they were quick off the mark they might run into a gang, if not they would encounter a blood-soaked clearing in the forest, piled high with gore, wherein as many animals as was practical had been slaughtered and the meat hurriedly bundled and carried off.

In due course Tracker Combat Units came of age. Peter Hewitt's team was known for the purpose as Tracker Combat Unit No. 9. The key point is that Combat Tracker Teams, notwithstanding relying heavily on recent captures for intelligence and active assistance on patrols, were not attempting to present themselves as enemy combatants and so where as such not pseudos.

> Between follow-ups and routine patrols around the forest edge my team always made a diligent practice of thoroughly interrogating all terrorists either captured or surrendered that we could lay hands on. Immediately they put in an appearance at the station a request was lodged to use them. Sometimes they were whisked straight off to the inner sanctums of Special Branch and would not be seen again for days, often to re-appear as pseudo gangsters and inducted into the Field Intelligence Officer's group. At other times they would be sent direct to those security forces responsible for the area in which they had been sallying to and fro as an active forest gangster.[34]

This had been precisely the mantra that Frank Kitson repeated time and again in terms of the most optimum use of turned guerrillas in pseudo gangs. Surely it would have made indisputable sense for pseudos to be sent back to re-engage precisely with those wandering gang members whom they had been among only days previously However, as Kitson set sail for Malaya, no doubt to apply there much that he had learned in Kenya, he was wont to shake his head at the monolithic resistance to innovation that tends to afflict any army's central command, although at this point it hardly mattered; the war, such as it was, was as good as won. There was just one key piece of business left to take care of before matters could finally be laid to rest.

CHAPTER SEVEN:

THE HUNT FOR DEDAN KIMATHI

"I am a great warrior ever owned by Africans and have offered not for Kenya alone but for East Africa and Africa as well ..."
—*Dedan Kimathi*

By December 1955 the rate of defections, surrenders and captures had diminished to a trickle. In the vast Aberdare region it had been estimated that less than 1,500 guerrillas remained active. The security threat represented by this had diminished to almost nil. Mau Mau had been downgraded to the level of a public nuisance, rendering it wholly irrelevant to the new political process that continued under the leadership of such names as Jomo Kenyatta, Tom Mboya, James S. Gichuru and Oginga Odinga. Even Waruhiu Itote, the evergreen General China, would find a berth in the independent government as a junior minister and a character at large. However, the most powerful personality in the movement, Dedan Kimathi, remained unaccounted for. Kimathi appeared to be something of a Colonel Walter E. Kurtz in his own savage, green kingdom, his sanity disintegrating daily, his dream of pan-Africanism crumbling in his hands and his lofty preoccupations being reduced to the basics of obsessive paranoia, fervent supernatural communion and retributional murder.

This image of Dedan Kimathi was pervasive, and arguably the one most whites of the time preferred. It also happened to fit very well into the pattern of millennial revolutionary which was how, fundamentally, Kimathi tended to regard himself. His early life had been malfeasant, revealing him, although clearly highly intelligent, to be violent, untrustworthy and indolent. He was also, however, touched by a premonition of some sort of personal destiny. This was borne out to a degree by what he was able to achieve as a guerrilla leader, but throughout his career he had seen himself as much more than this, as indeed a leader, not only of Kenya, but of Africa as a whole. His politicisation was certainly genuine, inasmuch as he had been personally touched by the inequities of a race-categorising system, and had felt the many pinpricks of prejudice and bigotry that were facts of life for any black person during the first half of the 20th century. However, although a zealot, he was hardly an ideologue in the true sense of the word, for he lacked both education and erudition.

Beyond these shreds of uncontested detail very little is actually known about Kimathi, and since his most intellectually fertile

Kuri Atongoria othe a Mau Mau na Arumiriri ao

MAUNDU MERU MA KWINEANA

Riri ni Ihinda Ria Kuhonokia Muoyo Waku!

RIU NI IHINDA RIAKU UHONOKIE MUOYO WAKU

NDUNGICIIRITHIO NI UNDU WA IHITIA RIA MAU MAU O NA RIMWE RIRIA URIKITIE GWIKA MBERE YA KIRIKANIRO GIKI —UGUO NI KUUGA, KUUMA MUTHENYA WA JANUARY 18, MWAKA WA 1955. UGUO NI GUKWIRA ATI NDUNGICIIRACWO KANA UITWO NI UNDU WA UMARAMARI ONA URIKU URIA URIKITIE GWIKA MBERE. UTANGIKORUO NIUGWIKA UURU UNGI THUTHA WA MUTHENYA UCIO.

GENERAL SIR GEORGE ERSKINE,
Mutongoria Mumene wa Ita.
Muthenya wa January 18, Mwaka wa 1955.

SIR EVELYN BARING,
Barathi wa Kenya.

Above: Leaflet calling on Mau Mau to surrender, air-dropped into the forests.

Right: An elderly tribesman is fingerprinted.

years were spent surrounded by ignorance and illiteracy, it is only through the highly partisan accounts of both friends and enemies that one can hope to paint a more detailed portrait of who and what Dedan Kimathi was.

One such comment that will give the reader a clear sense of how Kimathi might have been regarded by the wider security establishment at the time was made by the co-writer of Ian Henderson's account of his hunt for Dedan Kimathi, Sir Philip Goodhart, a British politician and MP, when he wrote: "If the Kikuyu were the Germans of tribal Kenya, [then] Kimathi was their Hitler."[12]

Goodhart then goes on, as, throughout the preamble to the book he sketches the life and character of Kimathi, to construct a picture of a man absolutely devoid of virtue. He does accurately point out, and this is perhaps where the allusion to Hitler fits in most comfortably, that Kimathi was also a seductive and passionate orator, who, when stimulated by an acute ideological identification became almost irresistible to his followers.

Needless to say Goodhart's profile of Ian Henderson in the same narrative is warmly congratulatory and rich with the merits of a true white son of Africa. Henderson certainly did win a great deal of approbation from his colleagues during those thrilling days of the chase, and he continued to enjoy the admiration of his peers for a long time afterwards. However, the latter phases of his career appear to have been blighted by accusation of torture and brutality associated with his 30-year contract as a high-ranking security service functionary in Bahrain. This phase of his career led to the less than flattering epithet, 'The Butcher of Bahrain', for which Henderson is now better known than for any work that he might have done in Kenya. There have been wide-ranging calls for Henderson to be brought to account for his complicity in torture and the abuse of prisoners both in Kenya and elsewhere, which creates some difficulty in reconciling this *wunderkind* of colonial Kenya with such a beast of the post-colonial period. A similar conundrum no doubt plagues those currently attempting to reconcile Kimathi, 'The Hitler of the Kikuyu', with the legacy of a man whose bronze statue is today featured prominently in downtown Nairobi, and whose credibility among the revolutionary heroes of Kenya, and indeed of the entire black diaspora, remains impeccable.

The question of how to track down and destroy Dedan Kimathi became something of an obsession for Ian Henderson. By the end of 1955 he could claim more direct experience of Mau Mau hunting in the dark recesses of the Aberdare forests than any other white man in the security services. This is evidenced by the fact that, despite being outranked, he was included in a *troika* of experts charged with developing a strategy to isolate and capture or kill Dedan Kimathi. The other two were Assistant Commissioner John Prendergast and Superintendent Anthony Lapage.

The problem that the three men faced was that Kimathi had not successfully remained one step ahead of security forces by being a fool. He had so far evaded every trap that had been laid, and was wise to just about every established tactic that the pseudo groups had developed. Coupled with this, no one knew with any certainty where Kimathi was in the vast interior of the Aberdare Forest, and

[12] Many writers of the period have made reference to the Kikuyu as the Germans of black East Africa, thanks to their industry, resourcefulness and entrepreneurial instinct.

A Mau Mau is captured by British troops in the forest.

British Army soldiers by their Land Rover during operations in the Highlands.

with so few guerrillas still at large, most of whom would by then have known one another either by sight or reputation, and moreover were scattered over such a wide area, that it would be extremely difficult to get close enough to Kimathi to pin him down.

After many hours of discussion in the smoke-filled operations room at the Nyeri HQ the question was distilled down to one simple if implausible strategy: the only possible way of whittling away the protective layer that Kimathi had built about himself was to do so using loyal and trusted members of his inner circle. This was asking a great deal, however, since Kimathi, famously paranoid and dangerous to boot, kept company only with those who enjoyed his absolute trust, while others, all of whom were among the hardcore, knew that even the faintest trace of treachery would result in prompt execution. Kimathi had murdered those close to him countless times before, even some among his own blood relatives, and he would continue to do so until he had almost entirely exhausted his following.

The plan that was devised was necessarily simple, and would ultimately rely more on operational skill than brilliant planning. Members of Kimathi's inner circle needed to be coaxed out into the open and captured, and then quickly turned to lead a pseudo team back into the forest. After much discussion it was decided that three letters would be written, each addressed to Kimathi, and each offering terms of surrender.

The written word was in fact one of very few weaknesses the in Mau Mau armour. Without radio communications all messages and dispatches were distributed in written form. For this purpose Mau Mau used a system of post boxes, or *postas*, where letters were left and collected. *Postas* for Mau Mau couriers were like waterholes for wild animals. It was there that they were forced at some point or another to make an appearance, and it was there that the predators could almost certainly be found. The protocols of using the *posta* system were therefore extremely arcane, sometimes as minute as the direction of a blade of grass, or the placement of a rock.

Here, the small planning committee agreed, would be the most likely point of initiating contact with Kimathi's gang. Alongside the letters would be a sky shout advertising the location. If Kimathi's curiosity could be stimulated he would send a younger follower down the mountain to collect the letter. Long-term ambushes would be in place to apprehend an approaching guerrilla, or alternatively to make the capture after the letter had been retrieved, and at a point when one or more guerrillas was returning to post a reply.

Towards the end of December 1955, Henderson and Lapage entered the Aberdare Forest in order to plant the letters. Not one of these actually reached Kimathi, however, or any other of the surviving leadership, but an unexpected result was achieved by the sky shout. The message was heard by two high-ranking guerrillas, both fugitives from Kimathi, who concluded that surrender to the authorities carried less risk than capture by Kimathi. It must be stressed here that infighting within Mau Mau had by then claimed a great many lives, exacerbated by the rapid expansion of pseudo operations that had had the effect of completely shattering any internal cohesion and spreading suspicion and paranoia throughout the movement.

Contact was specifically made with Ian Henderson and a meeting arranged on a rain-soaked forest track deep in the Aberdares. Initially, the meeting seemed inauspicious, since neither man had direct access to Kimathi, and indeed each could expect to be garrotted should he be so unfortunate as to fall into Kimathi's hands, but it was all that had been achieved, and possibly all under the circumstances that could be hoped for, and Henderson was determined to make the best of it.

The two men – Gati and Hungu – were taken in and pushed through the usual turning process which in this case was understood to be inevitable by both parties. Thereafter, the original plan was abandoned and another quickly formulated. While trust was building between Henderson, Lapage and the two surrenderees, it was decided that both would be sent back into the forest in order, in the first phase, to harvest at least a dozen fresh captures for the purpose of forming a pseudo team for the specific purpose of working towards contact with Kimathi. Both men had fallen foul of Kimathi on a minor procedural transgression, which in Kimathi's current frame of mind was grounds for execution, but not so much in the eyes of two other key leaders – Kahiu Itina and Chege Karobia – each of whom were understood to enjoy unrestricted access to Kimathi, and into whose gangs Gati and Hungu might possibly be insinuated, particularly if their operational credentials could be enhanced a little.

To achieve this Henderson arranged a second sky shout that broadcast the message that Gati and Hungu had been elevated to the top of the government's most wanted list, and that a bounty of £600 had been placed on each of their heads. This naturally had the twin effect of confirming to anyone that might have had doubts that Gati and Hungu were still very much operational, and moreover that they must have been responsible for some extraordinary action in order for them to have been singled out for such attention. Kimathi himself soon came to hear of the bounty offer, which piqued him somewhat, since until then he alone in the forest had had that distinction, but at the same time it presented a comfortable (for Henderson at least) political conundrum that forced Kimathi to rescind his death sentence on the two and elevate their status within the movement.

The plan thereafter was to capture either one or both of the two sub-leaders. How this was to be achieved no one could guess, but the business of building the team went ahead under the hope, and indeed the expectation, that something would turn up.

That something turned out to be a convenient prophecy issued by a high-ranking medium by the name of Kingori who was closely associated with Kahiu Itina. Prior to this, the two founding members of the team – Gati and Hungu – had been fortunate enough in their early return to the forest to capture enough disassociated guerrillas to make up the optimum two teams of six men each. Thereafter, exploratory missions into the Aberdares established and confirmed more or less the whereabouts of Kahiu Itina, but no intelligence had been unearthed to give any indication of the location of Chege Karobia and his gang, or, for that matter, of Kimathi. Another fortunate capture during early April 1956 was linked somewhat to Kahiu Itina and a short time later another more directly. It was Gati who first encountered the gangster leader, and all the anxieties of how he would be practically apprehended evaporated. The pseudos were made unexpectedly welcome by Kingori, the medium, who had experienced a dream during which *Ngai*, the Kikuyu god that lived on Mount Kenya, spoke to him, informing him that emissaries of peace would soon arrive among them, and who would then lead them to a place of safety. As a consequence, the bulk of the gang submitted to capture with absolute compliance, presenting Henderson and the Special Branch team with an early Christmas present.

Kahiu Itina and Kingori were themselves completely uncooperative in the matter of discussing Kimathi, his state of mind or his whereabouts. Once separated from the rest of the gang, however, and handed over to the police for processing, interrogations of others in the gang proceeded more easily, and a great deal of detailed, if somewhat fragmented, information was volunteered. In the end, however, very little practical intelligence was gained, other than perhaps that Kimathi had grown more isolated, more paranoid and suspicious, and subsequently more dangerous. The consensus appeared to be that Kimathi would

An RAF Lincoln bomber over the Aberdares. Aerial bombing proved ineffective.

Captured Mau Mau terrorists.

Peter Hewitt crouches by the remains of Mau Mau terrorists dispatched a few days earlier by a security-force patrol. The hyenas and vultures have had their gory fill. *Photo Peter Hewitt*

remain on the mountain to the last, and would be the last to be accounted for, if, indeed, he ever was. He remained protected by a fanatical hardcore of followers who, despite his violent and unpredictable nature, continued to place stock in his supernatural power and his by then prodigious instincts for survival. He had, moreover, put the word out that, thanks to the proliferation of pseudo gangs, and the fact that no one could be trusted, no matter who they were, he would summarily kill anyone he encountered. This, therefore, mooted any hope that either Kahiu Itina or Chege Karobia would be able to penetrate his inner circle, even had they been willing. Therefore, apart from a slightly more focused sector of operation, and the fact that one more key leader and his followers had been removed from the picture, very little in practical terms had been achieved.

Nonetheless the hunt resumed, this time under punishing conditions of heavy rainfall in an environment of cloying mud, trails churned up by wildlife moving down towards the flatlands and the deeper gorges restricted by rivers and streams in spate. *Oi, egunaga ki* ran the Kikuyu refrain. *What use is there is crying*? Two groups of eleven men each entered different sectors of the forest while Henderson and his small support team lingered on the edges, rendezvousing periodically, and for the remainder gnawing their fingernails as they waited. On the third day Gati returned with a wounded capture seized during a running firefight. It was established after questioning this man that Kimathi had been no more than five miles away during the encounter, and would quite obviously have heard the firefight in progress and would have immediately fled the area. A blind search of adjacent stands of forest followed but nothing was turned up.

Henderson, however, was not wholly disappointed. He had now made direct contact with Kimathi's gang, or least part of it, and he could guess from this, more or less, where within in the 6,000-square-mile Aberdare Forest his quarry was. Gati and his team, however, had been seen by Kimathi's men and could be identified, and so were reluctantly removed from the hunt. Those that remained active were learning from these small successes, and

Hewitt (left) warily views his Mau Mau capture, the self-styled 'Field Marshal' Mbaria Kanui, during Operation *Bullrush* in the Naivasha papyrus swamps, January 1956. *Photo Peter Hewitt*

modifying their tactics here and there as they went. Henderson, meanwhile, had recognised early on that there was no point in compromising the operation, or any part of it, by him being actively involved. Even with the best disguise in the world there was a limit to how much a white man could hope to blend into a Mau Mau gang. He remained on the sidelines, partly as a deeply interested observer and partly as the key strategist.

It must be stressed that what made Henderson such a natural at this game was that he could think like a black man. This was a terrible cliché in Kenya at the time. Almost every white man who had been in the colony for more than two years felt similarly satisfied that he knew how the black man thought, but in reality very few did, even among those old hands who had been in Kenya for many years. Henderson appears to have used a simple formula in dealing with his pseudos. He recognised that it was they who would be at the cutting edge of every operation, and he was cognisant of the fact that they knew both the terrain and the mindset of the fugitive gangsters far better than he. He tended to plan first in broad brushstrokes within his committee, after which the general outline of a plan was handed to the relevant team, leaving it thereafter to them to sit around in a tight circle and debate the practicalities until they were ready to act.

> The brains behind the whole show were the converted Mau Mau themselves. They were undoing the bolts in the evil Mau Mau machine which they themselves had constructed. They knew where the nuts were, and they had the tools to do the job.[35]

This was arguably the key to operating a successful pseudo unit, certainly if Henderson was to have any hope of closing with one of very few remaining Mau Mau with any appetite left for the struggle. Kimathi was no ordinary prey, and although a good deal of luck had so far influenced the picture in Henderson's favour, luck alone would not bring Kimathi in. Perseverance, cold cunning and excellent man-management were the key strengths that Henderson brought to the contest, which, in a strange way, were precisely those Kimathi employed to evade him. Kimathi, however, also had superstition and terror. If Henderson happened to lack the former, he could at the very least understand it, and although he might have been legally restrained from exercising the latter, there has never been any doubt that he was quite capable of it.

Meanwhile, luck remained on the side of the pseudos. A few weeks later a fresh snare was encountered where a patient ambush yielded two fresh captures, both members of Kimathi's gang. According to Henderson, "These were the exact circumstances for which we had prayed. This was the type of quiet operation, the 'snatch', which would bring Kimathi's men secretly into our hands."[36]

Subsequent interrogations revealed that Kimathi had been shaken by the earlier contact and had fled the sector, dividing his 49-strong group into three sub-groups, himself moving off in the company of just 15 men. He had warned the remainder not to leave the area, and to send word to him as soon as it was safe. The two trappers had been separated by some distance from their main

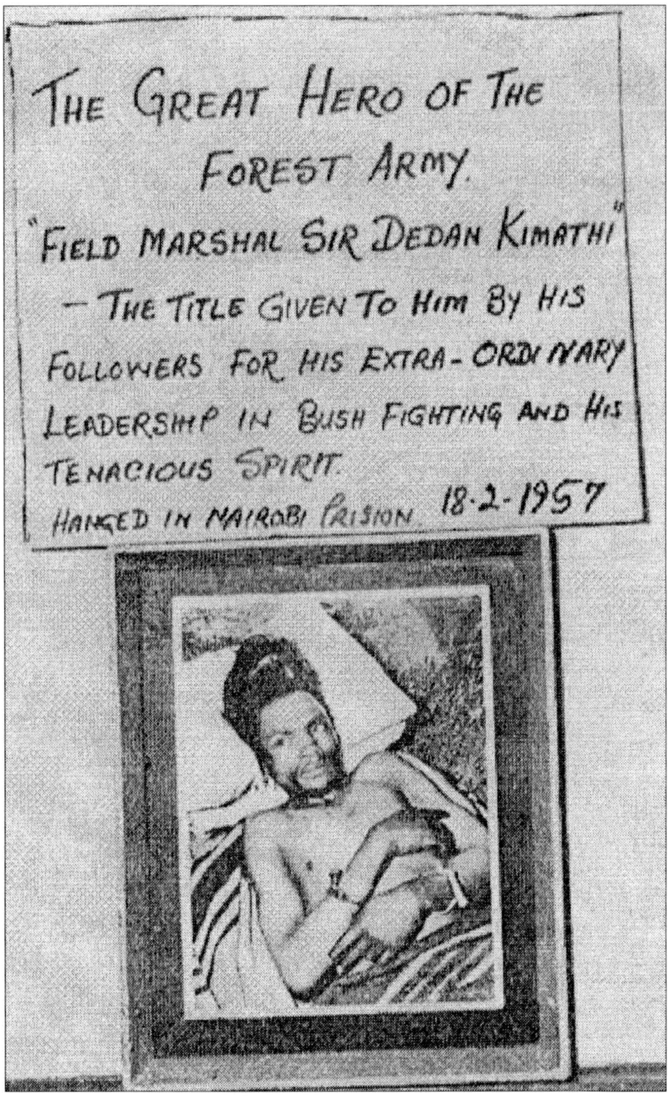

A newspaper cutting depicting a framed photograph of the celebrated Mau Mau leader. Dedan Kimathi, lying manacled in a Nairobi hospital bed following his capture. Above is a home-made commemorative plaque.

group, presenting the opportunity to turn them and get them back into the forest quickly before any suspicion could set in that they had been captured.

And so it was. The hunt continued with no fresh leads on the whereabouts of Kimathi but with ongoing attrition gradually diminishing the numbers of guerrillas available for him to call upon. Substantial contact was not made again until early June 1956 when a handful of Kimathi's men were tracked back into the forest after foraging potatoes in a native reserve garden plot. The follow-up resulted in the capture of five guerrillas including Kimathi's brother.[13] More valuable information accrued and the closer to Kimathi Henderson crept.

There were by then almost a hundred pseudos operating in the Aberdares, with the core group still actively hunting Kimathi. Success bred success, as Henderson noted: "A hostile gang fighting us yesterday became a tamed gang fighting for us today."[37] The turnaround was so quick and the technique now so finely tuned that pseudo gangs were able to merge quickly and

The CO of the Glosters confers with his second-in-command at TAC HQ during Operation *Bullrush* in the Naivasha papyrus swamps.

easily with fugitive gangs, and equally quickly compromise them and bring them in. Week by week the exponential growth of the pseudo gangs mirrored the decline of Mau Mau, and each week the noose tightened around Kimathi's neck. It remained a cat and mouse game with luck still the defining influence.

Of course, not all guerrillas captured during the operation were seconded into pseudo groups. Screening would weed out those irredeemable among the captures from those with worthwhile information and an apparent willingness to share it.

> Those who were suspected of committing specific atrocities or major crimes were handed over to the authorities with the least possible delay to stand trial; those against whom no definite charge could be made, but who were, nevertheless, particularly bad characters, were sent off to detention. Some, we felt, would respond to civilisation fairly quickly, others might take longer, others would probably never respond. They would remain a menace to society as long as they lived.[38]

This separation of bad from worse, as Henderson put it, was always done with care, with particular emphasis on those appearing to be willing to switch allegiance. Again, as Henderson notes, "We were trying to persuade them to change their regiment, not their souls."[39] The main risk, however, the same risk that future generations of pseudo handlers in Mozambique, Angola and Rhodesia would face, was that a person professing a change of regiment could in fact revert at the first opportunity, killing as many of those around him as he could. It happened very rarely and once the point had been reached that there were more pseudos in the forests than active Mau Mau, there was increasingly less to be gained by not responding to an offer to work with the government. Everybody by then recognised that it was a matter essentially of euthanising a movement that was manifestly bleeding to death anyway.

And while the pseudo teams and a much scaled-down military force continued to undertake the task of mopping up the remnants in the forest, they could do so in the certain knowledge that the Kenya Police, the Tribal Police Reserve and various Home Guard

[13] In African paternity it is common for the term brother or sister to be very loosely applied. In a polygamous environment varying ranks of sibling can range from children of the same parents to those of the same father but different mothers, to cousins within the extended family.

units had gained such a firm grip on the surrounding reserves that the mere appearance of a Mau Mau unit outside of the forest invited dispatch. Any guerrillas operating outside of the main forest blocs, and these were by then extremely rare, were being systematically dealt with by the FIAs and their pseudo groups.

This said, however, there were a few gangs that permanently based themselves in the reserves. These were described as reserve or settled-area terrorists, undertaking no direct offensive actions, but emerging from deep concealment only at night, and only to steal food. They subsisted in elaborate and brilliantly concealed underground hideouts and were not at all easy to locate. They presented no meaningful security risk and were dealt with via the usual avenue of police action, utilising a civilian population now more than willing, and indeed often quite happy, to provide the necessary intelligence.

The hunt for Kimathi, meanwhile, went on. All the certainties and predictabilities of mopping up the last of Mau Mau did not apply to him. The next substantive contact came about thanks to a rapid follow-up on an incident of stock theft that appeared to have been attributable to Kimathi's men. While this did not prove to be the case, two Kimathi men were nonetheless captured who indicated that the fugitive leader had been very close, but again had slipped away.

By then it was July 1956 and the long rains had come to an end. The forest was slowly drying out as winter temperatures plunged. On 4 July five members of Kimathi's gang were captured and another two killed. Guided by one of the captures another two were run to ground and captured. A fortnight later an important Kimathi sub-leader was captured. Two pseudos were killed, however, which brought the total to four, two having being killed earlier by a wounded buffalo. Needless to say, as soon as shots were fired Kimathi again melted away into the forest, lighter in entourage and exponentially more vulnerable. His gang was now down to 24 men with an estimated 250 rounds of ammunition between them. Matters for Kimathi were dire, but the chase continued.

Speculation among the pseudos dwelt on the possibility that Kimathi might kill himself rather than be captured, which would have been very difficult to prove had it happened, and certainly would have left the matter entirely unresolved. However, in early August, contact was once again made with Kimathi's gang, fleeting and inconclusive, during which, needless to say, Kimathi himself made good his escape. Two guerrillas were captured. Then later that month, Chege Karobia and four gang members were captured. In order to augment his own dwindling force Kimathi had some weeks previously absorbed Chege Karobia and his gang, so this was another landmark moment, inching the endeavour towards some sort of a conclusion. Chege proved to be a fountain of excellent intelligence but still not quite enough to produce a definitive contact with Kimathi.

By the beginning of September 1956, through a combination of captures, defections and executions within the group, Kimathi's strength had diminished to eight individuals, including a woman who had been his closest companion for several years. He was also by then one of only two substantive Mau Mau leaders left in circulation, the other being a certain Kimani Kimarua.[14] Kimani Kimarua was accounted for in a firefight with one of Henderson's pseudo teams, leaving Kimathi alone in an area that only three years earlier had harboured an estimated 12,000 guerrillas under some 200 major and minor leaders.[40] Now that Kimathi was the only guerrilla of any importance on the mountain it was decided to ignore the leaderless remnants of various gangs still clinging to survival in the forest and concentrate the entire force on the hunt for him.

An operation codenamed *Hot Scrum* was meticulously formulated to concentrate a large force at 14 key points in the forest where it was determined that sites of importance to Kimathi existed. On the evening of 7 October a large convoy of covered trucks began transferring the force from its base to the edge of the forest, reaching its destination by dawn. Two base camps were established from where, on 9 October, the force began to penetrate the forest, heading variously for identified prayer trees, food stores and trapping areas, with others placed in ambush positions at various points.

Henderson mooted this as a do-or-die operation. Kimathi was by then so isolated that it was quite probable he might begin to seriously consider suicide, or perhaps succeed in slipping away from the operational area altogether, merging into one of the populated regions or seeking isolation in the empty reaches of the Northern Territory. Henderson banked on the operational life for this exercise to be two weeks. Thereafter the forest would be so saturated by the tracks of the pseudo teams that any meaningful offensive activity would be pointless. In that eventuality, if they failed to bring Kimathi in, the hunt might well be over.

Days passed, with the search producing no results at all. Kimathi was nowhere to be found. Then, a week after the launch of the operation, a letter was intercepted from Kimathi, written in his own hand, offering no solid clues but indicating at least that he was still in the forest. Tracks were also being located here and there, while a brief and blind firefight in a dense riverine bog, choked with sedge grass and reeds, turned up a lightly wounded guerrilla identified as Gitahi, a very close confederate of Dedan Kimathi. Gitahi was turned there and then, after which he offered to lead the team to Kimathi's current location. Others of Kimathi's group had escaped, and Kimathi would be on the move the moment he became aware.

Upon this nail-biting pivot the work of the previous six months hung. Gitahi and his team, with Gitahi carried on a mocked-up bamboo stretcher, were the first out, moving rapidly up through the forest towards the site of Kimathi's last known hideout. There was obviously very little chance that Kimathi would be in

[14] Stanley Mathenge disappeared from the scene sometime in 1955. His fate has never been wholly established, with rumours later circulating that he was living in Ethiopia. On 30 May 2003 a man believed to be Stanley Mathenge, living in Ethiopia, was invited to Kenya by President Mwai Kibaki and was given a hero's welcome by the state. It was soon revealed that the man was Ato Lemma Ayanu, who himself denied being Mathenge. DNA tests published four years later proved he was not Mathenge

residence, but a fair chance at least that a rapid follow-up could run him to ground. And so it was. Just before nightfall the camp was located, but Kimathi had left; moreover, the care he had taken to cover his tracks suggested that he had not left in a hurry. However, the fact remained that he was nearby, and in the dwindling light a careful search continued. A short while later a second hideout was discovered, this time there remained a hastily abandoned if extremely meagre meal, and such vital items of survival equipment as trapping wire, a small cooking pot and Kimathi's tattered copy of the Kikuyu Bible: his worldly wealth in effect.

By then the various ambush teams had been mustered and reassigned in support of Gati and began to arrive on the scene the following morning. In the midst of all this a brief but extraordinary incident occurred. As a team under the command of a certain Ruku made their way up the mountain, Ruku himself injured his foot on a tree stump and fell back. As he was attending to the injury he glanced up to see Kimathi emerging into a clearing and standing for a moment in clear sight. Raising his sub-machine gun Ruku pulled the trigger, but the weapon failed. Alerted, Kimathi looked up and watched as Ruku cleared the weapon and fired again, and once more a light click announced a failure. Upon that Kimathi was gone.

To someone like Henderson this incident might have appeared merely as further proof of Kimathi's obscene good luck, but to the Kikuyu men pondering the news as it circulated it was a clear vindication of Kimathi's self-proclaimed immortality, or at the very least of his favoured status in the eyes of *Ngai*.

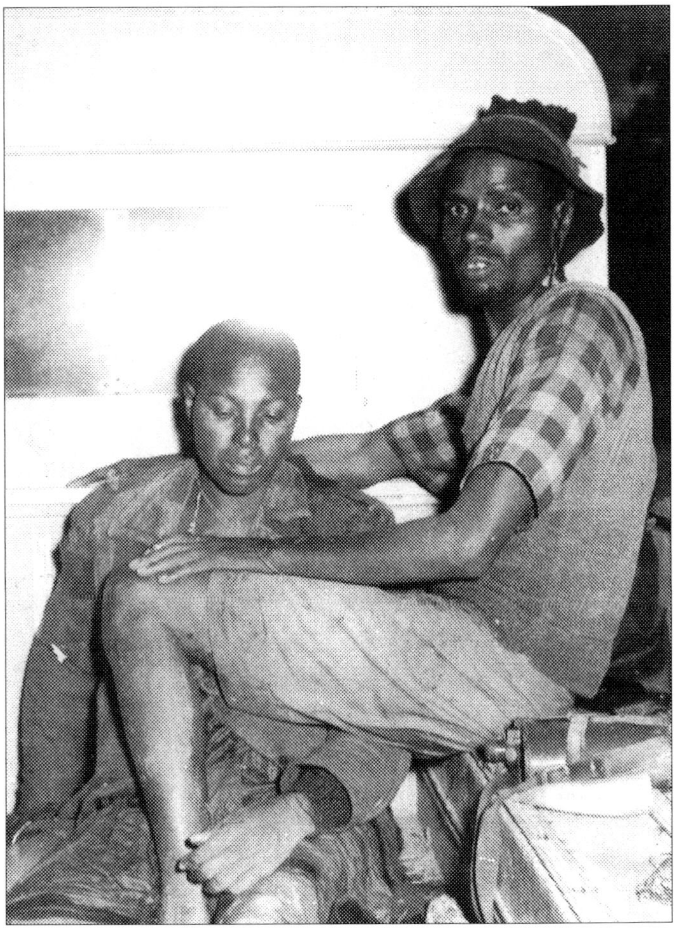

'Field Marshal' Mbaria Kanui, captured during Operation *Bullrush*. With him is his faithful forest concubine who had been shot and wounded in the thigh. He chose to stay with her in the swamps until capture rather than attempt a breakout.

There was, however, little time then to dwell on the incident. Events were moving quickly. In the company of two others, his female companion included, Kimathi was moving quickly through the forest, closely tailed by Gati and an advance section of his team, with additional teams closing in from other directions. Then another typically brief and confused firefight broke out that momentarily stunned the last of Kimathi's men, who then broke away leaving Kimathi alone with his woman.

The fugitive was intermittently seen by a number of his pursuers as he moved rapidly through the undergrowth, some of whom managed to fire a burst in his direction, but each time he managed to slip away. Then, as the running firefight began to dissipate, Kimathi's woman fell back and was captured, leaving him entirely alone.

Once again an operation was wound down with much attrition suffered by the enemy but still without that key success that would bring the whole matter to a satisfactory conclusion. It was fair at that point to conclude that it was only a matter of time. Kimathi would now have no choice but to either kill himself or somehow escape the forest. He had no means of feeding himself so would eventually, should he choose to live, have to leave the forest in search of food, and in the end, this is precisely how he was apprehended.

He was spotted by a detachment of native constabulary as he attempted to regain the forest after stripping sugar cane and unripe bananas from a tree, and was shot. Badly wounded he nonetheless was able to crawl back under cover of the forest, but was located and brought in some hours later. This conclusion might have seemed anti-climactic, but it fact it was the predictable conclusion of a text-book pseudo operation and would arguably remain the signature blueprint of successful operations of its kind from that point onwards.

The capture of Dedan Kimathi achieved many things. It definitively brought the entire chapter of Mau Mau to a close, marking a point at which offensive operations in the Aberdares ended. Mopping up continued, and the post-Emergency attempts at rehabilitation of Mau Mau and its affiliates went on for some time, which we will examine in the succeeding chapter, but the war, such as it was, was over.

It also had the less definable effect of securing the reputations of the two principal protagonists in the drama. Henderson found himself bathed in the accolades of his peers and others of the imperial establishment, while Kimathi emerged as a revolutionary hero, with the less palatable aspects of his character expunged, and his martyrdom displayed to the world at large through a dramatic trial and a prompt execution.

With the publication of Henderson's landmark book, *The Hunt for Kimathi*, in 1958, the episode was projected internationally very much to the taste of the wider reading public of the time, but certainly not in the manner that it would later be reinvented by the various governments of independent Kenya. Kimathi now stands in bronze replica in downtown Nairobi, clad in British-style military regalia, holding a rifle in his the right hand and a *simi* in the other, symbolizing the last weapons that he held, while his name now adorns schools, stadia and avenues throughout Kenya. Kimathi was a man of enormous courage and commitment, and that he also suffered from significant character flaws does not in any way exclude him from the club of great men throughout history. He was the most important leader of Mau Mau through whom the organisation came closest to being a centrally commanded army. That he failed ultimately in achieving the overall command structure that he sought speaks more of the failings of the organisation as a whole than of him as an individual. Had he enjoyed the advantages of Cold War patronage and Front Line support that some like Robert Mugabe or Samora Machel had access to there can be no doubt that he would have ranked among the highest achievers of the African liberation movement.

CHAPTER EIGHT:
REHABILITATION

A number of those captured during these closing stages of substantive operations were subsequently detained at Hola Camp, a detention centre situated in an unremarkable settlement on the Tana River, midway between the coastal idyll of Malindi and the somewhat less idyllic frontier town of Garissa. Hola Camp was one of a number of detention centres scattered around the colony for the purpose of what the colonial authorities termed Rehabilitation, a social engineering project, somewhat in keeping with the times, and which was rather a belated effort to help the Kikuyu in particular identify with the manifest inevitability of European political dominance, and to fast-track the emergence of a conservative, affluent and landed black middle class.

The Rehabilitation process owes its origins to the fundamental belief among those responsible for native affairs in the colony, which tended to cut across many local administrative departments, that Mau Mau was some kind of mass moral derangement premised on everything imaginable other than legitimate political aspiration. The level of violence and brutality that accompanied Mau Mau tended to reinforce this perception, striking fear into the hearts of temperate white observers, few of whom could imagine any possibility of responsible, mature government emerging under the tutelage of such a brace of bloodthirsty savages.

The idea of seeking a solution to the steadily amplifying calls for independence across British Africa by generating a black middle class was not unique to Kenya. Rhodesian Prime Minister Sir Edgar Whitehead sought a similar solution in what he termed Build a Nation, offering himself and his minority administration as a preferable option to the violent and unstable rule of local black nationalists, targeting his message to those blacks who could be judged to have most to lose from majority rule. These, naturally, would have been those with land and property, but they were small in number, and could only be relied upon to alter the political destiny of the territory if the franchise could be sufficiently restricted to exclude the vocal and militant black majority that continued to languish in poverty. However, by the time this realisation dawned it was largely too late to so radically alter the social landscape of Southern Rhodesia, as it was in Kenya at more or less the same time.[41]

The first tier of demographic control in Kenya, as it was all over the European colonial spectrum, was the pass laws. These at their most benign were identity papers which usually carried with them some sort of book or register that detailed a person's employment history as well as particulars of birth, age, marital status and gender. In most cases the objective of this was to monitor the movement of blacks, and to control their activities, or presence, within the main urban centres, which in most cases were statutorily exclusive to whites. Later, as insecurity mounted, these documents would be augmented by any number of separate passes allowing for movement between areas, employment here and there and security status in terms of what grade of risk an individual might have represented.

Prior to Operation *Anvil* the use of detention had neither been as intensely politicised nor as widely applied as it would later become. The declaration of a State of Emergency, however, widened the powers of the administration to make use of detention, which it did, in particular as it began to be assumed that detention could be applied both as a tool of social change as well as a weapon in the expanding counter-insurgency arsenal of the state. It might also be noted that it has been the detention and rehabilitation programme, perhaps more than any other aspect of Mau Mau that has left the British colonial reputation in tatters. Not only do a majority of simple abuse claims have their origins somewhere within the prison system, but the whole enterprise has an unpleasant Orwellian flavour, founded upon complete denial of black political capacity and informed by a wholly erroneous interpretation of the mood of the black population at large.

The first two camps to begin receiving political prisoners or detainees were Kajaido, a railway settlement south of Nairobi, and Athai River, more or less on the southern outskirts of Nairobi. As political dissent began to widely manifest itself in the colony these two facilities became noticeably more political in character, with both being in effect *de facto* rehabilitation centres by the end of 1953. The Rehabilitation system worked along the principle of a pipeline, into which subverted individuals were inducted and out of which reformed and responsible citizens would emerge. The process began at two large screening camps established at MacKinnon Road in the Coastal Province and Manyani, northwest of Nairobi. Here detainees were screened and classified as black, grey or white. Black implied the irredeemable loss of a soul to the heresy of nationalism, grey a possible ideological casualty requiring deeper observation and white those found after screening to be, if not loyal, then at least uninfected.

While 'blacks' were filtered out early and sent to special detention camps such as Hola or Mageta Island in Nyanza Province, the vast majority of detainees were classified as 'grey', and these were dispatched out to more than 45 detention or work camps distributed around the Central and Rift Valley provinces. It was deemed that they might be conditioned towards useful citizenship upon the application of certain moral stimulus. At its most basic

Literally thousands of suspects were rounded up for rehabilitation.

The Kamiritho protected village, little more than a concentration camp.

Governor Sir Evelyn Baring inspects troops during his 1959 farewell parade.

this was an acknowledgement, or confession, of association with or sympathy for Mau Mau, followed by a ceremonial denunciation of the oath (in certain instances Kikuyu elders or spiritualists were employed to enact rituals to achieve this) and the embrace of a 'superior idea'. Often this was accomplished through a 'break-'em-down-and-build-'em'-up programme based on an endlessly repeated censure of a person's perceived seditious views followed by the equally repetitive promotion of a superior ideal: Christianity leavened with imperialism being the usual choice.

According to Wunyabari Maloba, who cites a number of official documents as his sources, Kikuyu evangelists were seconded to many if not all detention camps and given a free hand in their activities. Any inmate who responded positively to this message was required to submit a written confession confirming his participation in oathing, and in return for a substantial reduction in his sentence, charged with the responsibility of spreading the word. As an adjunct to this, and aided considerably by the concentration of populations into protected villages, were confessional *barazas*, or councils, where those who had confessed were showcased at public meetings and there required to repeat their confessions to an audience of their peers. Others were encouraged to do likewise, some, who were named and called out, would later be subject to the usual process of screening at the hands either of loyalists or Special Branch.[42]

Besides this the work-camp regime was semi-military in character with manual labour being required under the general notion that idleness stimulates cogitation which in turn generates resentment and antipathy. Much of this work was community-oriented, although public works were also undertaken, the Embakasi, or Jomo Kenyatta International Airport being one such construction project where work-camp labour was applied. If a detainee was found to be progressing well a slight easing of conditions might have been offered in the form of transfer to a detention camp closer to his village or home area. Usually this type of assessment was made after referral to established loyalists who toured the various detention camps as government agents. These men were used in interrogations and various other screening processes to help establish the degree to which an individual had been rehabilitated.

The whole process was modelled quite closely on a similar system used in Malaya, which in turn drew inspiration from earlier programmes used in Greece and Palestine. The project was coordinated by a local official, the Commissioner of Community Development, who in this case was Thomas Askwith, a progressive Afrophile who served in East Africa in many socially oriented portfolios, ending his career as British Permanent Secretary in the Ministry of African Affairs. Askwith toured Malaya in the company of Sir Gerald Templar, architect of the local hearts and minds programme, learning from Templar the importance of the interrelated concept of rehabilitation and resettlement, realising from this that rehabilitation alone would amount to nothing more than a monumental waste of time and money. It was also Askwith who put forward the concept of drawing from indigenous traditions and rituals in order, one supposes, to fight fire with fire. In this regard he worked with the famous East African archaeologist Louis Leakey in formulating a culturally sensitive means for a Kikuyu man or woman to confess that he or she had participated in Mau Mau oathing.[43]

Detention and work camps, alongside the villagisation programme, both with absolute institutionalised control, represented the stick component of rehabilitation, while resettlement, training and other rewards of repentance represented the carrot.[15] Needless to say the process was steeped heavily in favour of loyalists, which, as was the case with the entire business, tended to represent a very heavy-handed and rather ill-informed intrusion into an already burdened native land-tenure system. As was often the case within the colonies, these grand schemes were implement based on the notion of some technocrat or other, and usually informed by an imperfect understanding of the local dynamics and deeper and more entrenched native traditions. The programme in this case was termed the Swynnerton Plan in recognition of Roger Swynnerton, an official within the Department of Agriculture.

As something of a subtext to the idea of institutionalised land reform in Kenya, it ought to be noted that by the mid-1950s and early 1960s the reality of the land crisis in the colonies had become widely appreciated. In most cases early European land alienation was premised on the fact that a very insubstantial native population existed to contest any white land claims. By the middle part of the 20th century, however, massive population expansion, and the complete inability of pioneer period native reserves to absorb the demands of subsistence agriculture, created the urgent necessity for a re-evaluation of the native reserves. This was certainly the case in Southern Rhodesia, a colony that shared many characteristics with Kenya, insofar as both had large settler communities and both were heavily invested in European commercial agriculture. In the case of Southern Rhodesia the Native Land Husbandry Act, tabled in 1951, sought to control and limit land utilisation in the reserves with a view to weaning native farmers away from a subsistence mentality and towards more productive, sustainable and profitable commercial agriculture.

The basic premise of this was that those willing and able to farm using modern and rational practices would be given land, while those deemed wasteful and primitive would find themselves eventually landless. The understanding that underwrote what ultimately became one of the most divisive and hated aspects of colonial legislation was that a black industrial proletariat would emerge alongside a modern social state responsible for the care and maintenance of its citizens. Neither bore fruit, however, mainly because, on the one hand, white policy makers underestimated the black commitment to the land and on the other because statutes limiting black entry and settlement in urban areas tended to undermine the ability of blacks to leave the rural areas and settle in the cities.

In Kenya the parallel process, although perhaps not originally intended as such, was ultimately much more political in character. The Swynnerton Plan, within the context that it was tabled, came as a godsend for the established loyalist community. In essence the plan envisioned the consolidation and enclosure of a multitude of fragmented and scattered communal landholdings into productive plots sufficient to sustain an average native family and the production of a commercial surplus. These would, by necessity, be progressive farmers – "able and energetic Africans," as Swynnerton himself projected – capable of embracing the concept of commercial agriculture within a cash economy.[44] The major benefit of the plan would be the fact that individual landholders – the bedrock of the new middle class – would own a title deed on their property which would unlock development capital in the form of credit reserves that had been previously unavailable. The question, of course, was what process of selection would identify progressive farmers and filter out those that were not progressive. Under such intensely political circumstances as afflicted the Central Highlands at that time it is not hard to imagine that a basic distinction of loyalist against non-loyalist would deeply influence the process.

Loyalist Kikuyu immediately embraced the prospect of land redistribution as a windfall opportunity, and urged the government to aggressively pursue the program. Land seizure, it was mooted, would be the most severe punishment that could be inflicted on a Mau Mau sympathiser. In the words of the Special Commissioner for Central Province: "Thus land consolidation was to complete the work of the Emergency: to stabilize a conservative middle class, based on the loyalists; and, as confiscated land was to be thrown into the common land pool during consolidation, it was also to confirm the landlessness of the rebels."[45]

In fact, in the final analysis, land seizures as such were significantly less widespread than were rumoured, and were halted by the Crown in 1955 for obvious reasons, but the tremors that were felt as a consequence in the detention camps added a great deal of momentum to movement through the pipeline. Detainees hearing about what was afoot in the reserves feared not unreasonably that they were about to lose their land, prompting many to fast-track their own rehabilitation in the hope of escaping the system and returning to the land in order to be on hand to contest any effort to dispossess them.

So while loyalists were thwarted somewhat in this great opportunity, they still retained enormous influence over the fate of suspects within the pipeline system. Open camps were the last phase of the rehabilitation programme, and although significantly less restrictive, were still governed essentially by loyalists upon whose approval or disapproval the fate of any individual within the system hung. No release was effected without the endorsement of loyalists. And even then the conduct and adjustment of an individual was closely monitored by probation officers who worked directly with chiefs and loyalists, both of whom retained a great deal of influence over the future of any individual attempting to emerge from the system.

---

15 Other methods of collective punishment included land and livestock seizures as well as the closing of local markets.

The rehabilitation programme came to an abrupt end in March 1959 when the commandant of Hola Camp, a certain G.M. Sullivan, was confronted one morning by a corps of hardcore detainees who were unwilling to concede to the forced labour requirements of the system and staged a sit-down protest. What followed has become one of those signature events tossed back and forth between British Government supporters and detractors like a ping-pong ball. What is known, however, is that Sullivan ordered a stringent reaction to this act of insubordination; so much so that once the political debris had cleared it was revealed that eleven inmates had been clubbed to death. Initial efforts to cover up the incident did nothing but confirm official culpability. In an effort to limit the fall-out and salvage the tattered reputation of the entire post-insurgency response, detention camps all over the country were closed and the vast majority of detainees released soon afterwards.

A year later the State of Emergency was lifted and the matter officially laid to rest. At a cost of some £55 million to the local and metropolitan treasuries, and the lives of over 12,000 Kenyans of every stripe, the Mau Mau revolt was officially over.

CHAPTER NINE:

LEGACY OF MAU MAU

"We cannot deny that a great impetus was given to the national movement for independence by events of and after 1952"
—*The KANU Manifesto for Independence Social Democracy and Stability 1960/61*

Soon after Jomo Kenyatta's landslide victory in the first general election in Kenya held under the terms of an independence constitution, a ceremony was held in Nyeri to officially welcome Mau Mau out of the forests. The year was 1963, three years after the lifting of the State of Emergency, and seven years after the capture of Kimathi. The whole business was richly symbolic – restrictions had been lifted some time earlier and free movement between the reserves and the forests now largely unhindered – allowing those remaining technically unaccounted for to maintain that their war did not end until independence was achieved, and moreover, allowing Mau Mau as a movement to claim some part in the final push towards independence.

For Kenyatta himself, however, the event was rather awkward. The official position since 1952 had been that Kenyatta was leader of Mau Mau, backed up by the Corfield Report which also made this claim. Kenyatta, however, had very carefully avoided any direct association with Mau Mau, although a necessary ambiguity had accompanied his official denials, bearing in mind the possible future political value of Mau Mau, or perhaps more accurately the potential future political damage of overtly disowning Mau Mau.

Then, as the first Prime Minister of an independent Kenya, removed now from the comfortable immunity of opposition, Kenyatta found himself confronted with the legacy of a conflict that had only narrowly avoided the definition of a Kikuyu civil war, but which had felt like that to many of the people who had been directly affected. In his speech to the returning veterans Kenyatta made heavy use of the verbiage of forgiveness and reconciliation, aiming this primarily at his own people – and while acknowledging the part that the Land Freedom Armies had played in the liberation struggle, it is noteworthy that he had made absolutely no mention of Mau Mau during his lengthy speech delivered on Independence Day, and certainly thereafter he offered the movement no specific rights or any promise of compensation.

In private Kenyatta appeared to be even less sympathetic than this. In his 1968 autobiography, *Suffering without Bitterness*, he made the comment: "Mau Mau was a disease which had been eradicated, and must never be remembered again."[46]

This hardly acknowledges revolutionary legitimacy, and in fact is more reminiscent of those architects of the rehabilitation campaign who advocated the view that Mau Mau was some kind of collective possession, requiring a moral exorcism. Historians have made the point that this view had the effect of liberating the outgoing colonial regime from conceding that Mau Mau had represented any legitimate political grievance, thereby releasing those guilty of the dispossession and disenfranchisement of the majority of any wrongdoing.

Did Kenyatta and others of his political class wish to make the same point? Or could it have been simply the fact that the forest fighters on the whole represented the illiterate class of Kikuyu peasantry: odorous, unkempt, atavistic and unacceptably violent? Could it also have been true that too overt an acknowledgement of Mau Mau would have brought to the surface the fact that Mau Mau had been largely a Kikuyu enterprise, emphasising the uncomfortable fact that the Kikuya as a group had more or less achieved independence single-handedly, and further highlighting the fact that the Kikuyu were without doubt leading the pack in the race for high political office and the significant material benefits of independence?

At the time all of the above were true. For the sake of broader political reconciliation across the ethnic spectrum in Kenya, and indeed for more localised reconciliation within the Kikuyu tribe itself, it was necessary not to celebrate the existence of Mau Mau too loudly. This, of course, would in due course change, for as Kenyan author and scholar Munyabari O Maloba wisely notes: "Over time there emerges what can be termed the official version of events, which then constitutes the acceptable legacy of the liberation movement."[47]

This, of course, is absolutely true, not only in Africa but in any situation where a highly doctrinaire revolution succeeds in unearthing an entirely new epoch. The liberation period in Africa has been replete with such events, each in one way or another

A jubilant Kenyatta parades through Nairobi after his swearing-in as prime minister in December 1963.

Jomo Kenyatta in 1963, with a Mau Mau leader.

Tom Mboya, a Luo, acknowledges the crowd after being elected in his KANU constituency. Widely expected to succeed Kenyatta, he was, however, assassinated on a Nairobi street in 1969. There was considerable enmity between Kenya's two largest tribes, the Kikuyu and the Luo.

The statue of Dedan Kimathi in Nairobi.

Kenyan independence, 1963. The Duke of Edinburgh (left) next to Kenyatta at the formal celebrations.

setting the tone for the nation state that would emerge, and in many cases solidifying the right of the revolutionaries to be the architects of the peace, and thereafter the leaders of government into perpetuity. Moreover, as Maloba goes on to observe, the official version of events tends to be organic, growing and adapting to the ongoing needs of the revolution, and often doing so to further reinforce the claims to power of the architects of change once their democratic legitimacy has faded.

The difficulty with any discussion of Mau Mau as a liberation movement has been the fact that it was not, strictly speaking, the instrument that brought independence into being. It is also arguable whether armed revolt advanced the cause of independence, or indeed retarded it, bearing in mind that in the aftermath of the Second World War the British political establishment had already acknowledged the inevitability of decolonisation. Britain did, however, require that the process be peaceful and orderly, necessitating, in the cases of Kenya, Nyasaland and Northern Rhodesia among others, that overt civil disturbances accompanying the legitimate political aspirations of the people be suppressed before the necessary constitutional changes were negotiated and implemented. It is therefore not inconceivable that if the colony had not been under the terms of a State of Emergency throughout the 1950s, independence might have been implemented in Kenya a few years earlier.

The post-independence leadership of Kenya, notwithstanding paying a certain amount of lip service, has been noticeably remiss in affording Mau Mau the kind of institutionalised recognition and respect offered, for example, to the liberation movements of Mozambique and Zimbabwe. No senior Mau Mau personalities were involved in the constitutional negotiations that led to independence and, apart from General China, and even he very modestly, none assumed high office in any independence cabinet. This, again, points to a certain amount of elitism within the struggle. Mau Mau, as previously iterated, was a peasant revolt, undertaken by illiterate men and led in the field by others only marginally better educated. The political leadership, on the other hand, in particular those that had been conveniently incarcerated during the most bloody days, were educated men with clear political positions at a time when Africa, and Africans, placed perhaps an exaggerated importance on education and erudition. This brought to the fore of the struggle such men as Léopold Sédar Senghor, Félix Houphouët-Boigny, António Agostinho Neto, Robert Mugabe and many others whom Kenyatta could have greeted as equals, but among whom General China and Dedan Kimathi would have been an embarrassment.

Another factor that has lingered alongside and in no small part influenced the legacy of Mau Mau, has been the question of whether the movement was narrowly tribal in character or whether it was indeed a movement of national liberation. By far the majority of those that fought in the forests from 1952 to 1956 were Kikuyu, with a very minimal presence of other language groups such as the Embu, Meru and Kamba. The revolt also did not expand beyond the Central Province, precipitating absolutely no meaningful militant response anywhere else in the country. While it need not follow that simply because a liberation struggle is narrowly supported it is narrowly defined. Kimathi is known to have thought in terms of national liberation, and attempted to engage others in this wider concept of the struggle, even though the vast majority of those involved saw matters in no wider

Mau Mau veterans at a post-independence rally.

enjoyed very little authentic unity at any time, even during its active phase. A great deal of internal healing would have been required before any kind of common bond could evolve among Mau Mau veterans, and it is arguable whether this has ever been achieved at all.

perspective than what concerned them on a village or district level. Operation *Anvil* effectively severed the movement from any active political wing, besides which Mau Mau tended to miss the point of revolution – that it is 'of the people and for the people', and cannot therefore be separated from the wider political objective of the struggle. To many in the forests, particularly in the early years, the fight was the business of Mau Mau while the politics was the business of the politicians. Subsequently, in the absence of political direction, the movement was scuttled, lending some credibility to the official view of it as being a strictly localised civil disturbance configured along the lines of a criminal gangster organisation.

In independent Kenya the rehabilitation and reintroduction into mainstream society of Mau Mau veterans has tended also to be very slow to get off the ground. The matter has been tabled and debated often over the years, but broadly speaking avoided, with, until very recently, no officially recognised veterans' association or lobby group. The gap between the benefits accrued to the political elite through the achievement of independence and those accrued to ex-fighters is enormous. This then leads to the question of how those that survived the emergency regard themselves, and the end result of a struggle that was sold to them as a movement primarily to reclaim the land – hence the appellation Land Freedom Armies – which, for all intents and purposes, has been won back for the benefit of a narrow political and commercial elite. These may be predominately Kikuyu, allowing it at least to be said that arms were taken up by Kikuyu for Kikuyu, but an unavoidably cynical conclusion is there to be acknowledged by any that care to do so.

The fact that Mau Mau veterans have been unable to overcome this institutionalised reluctance to allow them to organise and evaluate their own contribution to the liberation struggle as a unified group, can be blamed somewhat on the movement itself, and the continuation of early tendencies towards fractured, disunited and ideologically uncertain leadership. In many respects this is hardly surprising if it is considered that, by 1956, a majority of forest fighters were working on the side of the colonial authorities, which can have no effect other than to fracture the unity of a movement that

A short word needs also to be added on what Mau Mau means to modern Britain, and the surviving residue of those Britons that confronted it. Nothing, of course, needs to be added to the tone of reportage in the immediate aftermath of Mau Mau, mainly from the European pen, but in later years, as the legacy of British colonialism has been submerged ever deeper under the disapprobation of history, Mau Mau has become simply another example of the arrogance, brutality and cruelty of the white man in Africa. The recent efforts by a number of surviving Mau Mau to extract compensation from the British Government for torture and abuse during the period, notwithstanding the resultant unearthing of fresh documentation on the suppression of Mau Mau, has tended to scratch at the scabs of an unhealed wound. Many surviving whites would doubtless utter in the privacy of their own circles that surely torture and abuse are relative, and that nothing ever done to Mau Mau by the incumbent authorities at the time could ever compare to what the Kikuyu did to each other? However, once again, it is through the prism of history that these things are judged, and currently, and arguably for the foreseeable future, it is unlikely that any white man of British descent would be permitted in a public forum to argue that Britain was justified in responding as it did to the multi-layered horror that also, inescapably, is part of the Mau Mau legacy.

In the final analysis, however, the ongoing debate surrounding Mau Mau can be distilled down to the simple question of whether the movement made any meaningful contribution to the independence of Kenya or not, and by its nature this debate will continue. The interpretation of history tends to reside with the literate, and sadly there were precious few literate Kenyans among those on the front line of the Land Freedom Armies. Oral accounts have a place in the formulation of history, but cannot really compete with the more virile interpretations written by scholars and many others who were not there. Definitive histories of Mau Mau from the point of view of those who fought against it abound, but almost nothing has been written by those who fought on the side of the movement itself.

APPENDIX

BRITISH UNITS INVOLVED IN THE KENYAN EMERGENCY

ROYAL AIR FORCE

No. 8 Squadron Vampire FB9
No.13 Squadron Meteor PR10
No. 49 Squadron Lincoln B2, stationed at Eastleigh; November 1953 to January 1954 & November 1954 to July 1955
No. 61 Squadron Lincoln B2, stationed at Eastleigh; March 1954 to June 1954
No. 66 Squadron
No. 100 Squadron Lincoln B2 stationed at Eastleigh; January 1954 to March 1954
No. 208 Squadron Venoms/Hunters, stationed at Eastleigh 1959 to1962
No. 214 Squadron Lincoln B2, stationed at Eastleigh; June 1954 to December 1954
No. 507 Squadron (telecommunications RAF), stationed at Eastleigh; 1960/61
1340 Flight, RAF

ARMY HQ EAST AFRICA COMMAND

39 Brigade
24th Flying Brigade
1st Battalion Duke of Wellington's Regiment
1st Battalion The XXth The Lancashire Fusiliers
1st Battalion The Black Watch (Royal Highland Regiment)
1st Battalion Royal Irish Fusiliers
The Buffs (Royal East Kent Regiment)
1st King's Own Yorkshire Light Infantry
The Devons (The Devonshire Regiment)
The Rifle Brigade

49 Brigade
HQ 49 Independent Infantry Brigade Signal Troop
1st Battalion The Royal Northumberland Fusiliers
1st Royal Inniskilling Fusiliers
1st King's Shropshire Light Infantry
1st Gloucestershire Regiment (April 1955 to April 1956 at Gil-Gil)

70 Brigade
2nd Coldstream Guards
2nd Battalion Scots Guards
3 Company Irish Guards
1st Battalion The Cameronians
3rd The King's Own Hussars
1st Battalion The King's Own Border Regiment
1st Battalion Royal Fusiliers
8th King's Royal Irish Hussars
Rifle Brigade
Durham Light Infantry
East African Independent Armoured Car Squadron
Gordon Highlanders
King's Regiment
The Staffordshire Regiment
The Kenya Regiment

Other

Royal Artillery
Royal Horse Artillery
One battery of East African Artillery, King's Shropshire Light Infantry
156 Battery East African Artillery
Royal Engineers
Royal Army Veterinary Corps
Royal Military Police
Women's Royal Army Corps

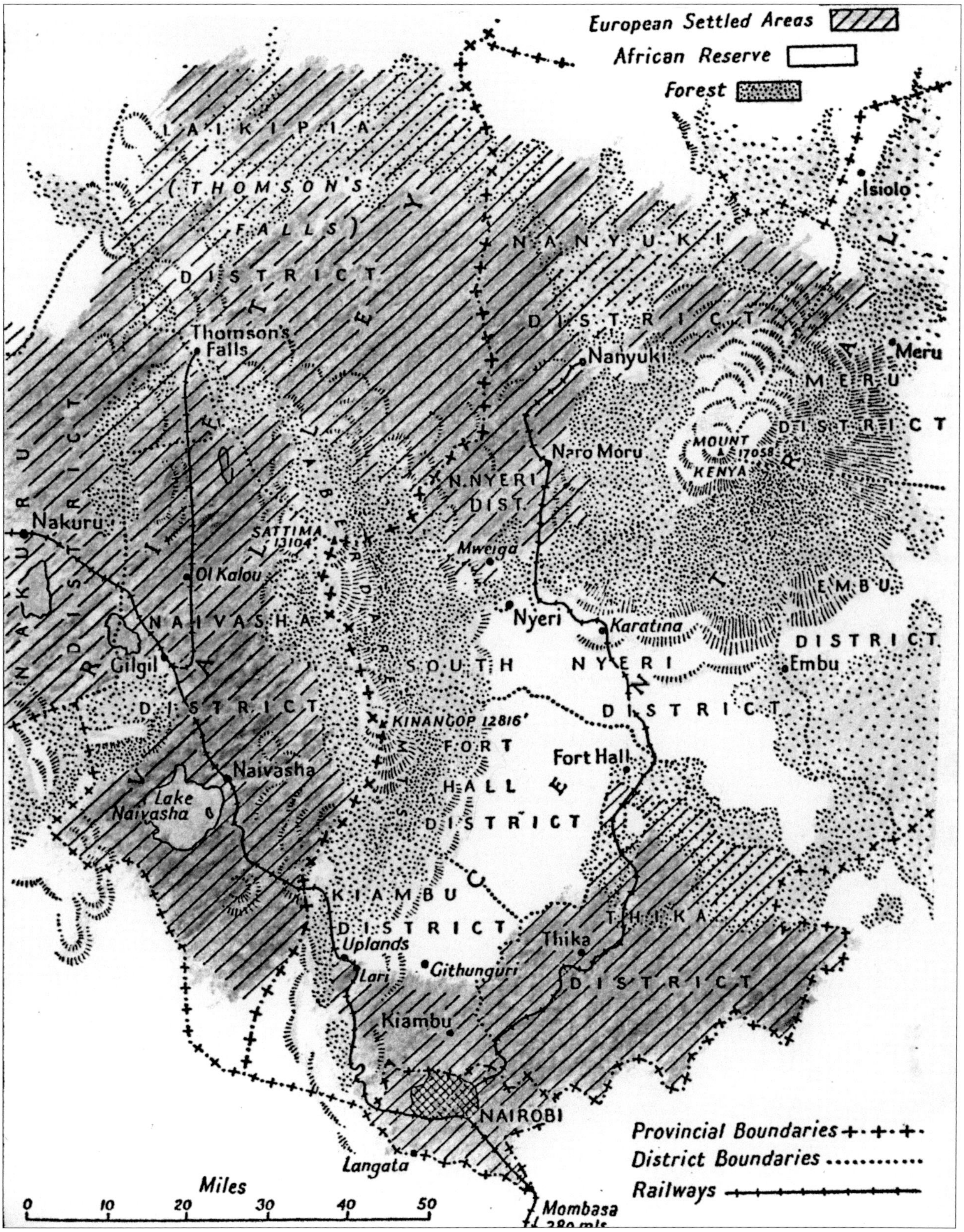

NOTES

1 Wikiquote
2 Majdalany, Fred. *State of Emergency: The Full Story of the Mau Mau.* (Haughton Mifflin Company, Boston, 1963) p. 11
3 Wilson, Christopher. *Kenya's Warning.* (English Press, Nairobi, Kenya, 1954) p. 10
4 Gray, Richard. *The Two Nations.* (Oxford University Press, London, 1960), p. 5
5 Maloba, Munyabari O. *Mau Mau and Kenya: An Analysis of a Peasant Revolt.* (Indiana University Press, Bloomington, 1998) p. 25
6 Quoted: Majdalany, Fred. *State of Emergency: The Full Story of the Mau Mau.* (Haughton Mifflin Company, Boston, 1963) p. 14
7 Quoted: Majdalany, Fred. *State of Emergency: The Full Story of the Mau Mau.* (Haughton Mifflin Company, Boston, 1963) p. 15
8 Kenyatta, Jomo. *Facing Mount Kenya.* (Vantage Books, New York, 1965) p. 22
9 Quoted: Majdalany, Fred. *State of Emergency: The Full Story of the Mau Mau.* (Haughton Mifflin Company, Boston, 1963) p. 57
10 Clayton, Anthony. *Counter-Insurgency in Kenya: A Study of Military Operations against Mau Mau 1952–1960.* (Sunflower University Press. Yuma, Manhattan, Kansas, 1984) p. 2
11 Kariuki (1960), p. 167
12 Kitson, Major Frank. *Gangs and Counter Gangs.* (Barrie & Rockliff, London, 1960) p. 45
13 Hearts and Minds, Psuedo Gangs and Counter Insurgency: Based upon Experiences from Previous Campaigns in Kenya (1952–60), Malaya (1948–60) & Rhodesia (1964–1979) Bill Bailey, Edith Cowan University
14 Quoted: Anderson, David. *Histories of the Hanged.* (W.W. Norton, New York 2005) p. 260
15 Quoted: Anderson, David. *Histories of the Hanged.* (W.W. Norton, New York 2005) pp. 299–300
16 Kitson, Major Frank. *Gangs and Counter Gangs.* (Barrie & Rockliff, London, 1960) p. 46
17 Anderson, David. *Histories of the Hanged.* (W.W. Norton, New York 2005) p. 241
18 Paget, Julian. *Counter Insurgency Operations.* (Walker, New York 1964) p. 75
19 Alao, Abiodub. *Mau Mau Warrior.* (Osprey Publishing, Oxford, 2006) p. 15
20 Wilson, Christopher. *Kenya's Warning.* (English Press, Nairobi, Kenya, 1954) p. 56
21 Hewitt, Peter. *Kenya Cowboy.* (30 Degrees South, Johannesburg, 2008) pp. 70–71
22 Hewitt, Peter. *Kenya Cowboy.* (30 Degrees South, Johannesburg, 2008) p. 160
23 Erskine, George. *Despatch to the Secretary of State for War,* 25 April 1955
24 Hewitt, Peter. *Kenya Cowboy.* (30 Degrees South, Johannesburg, 2008) p. 107
25 Hewitt, Peter. *Kenya Cowboy.* (30 Degrees South, Johannesburg, 2008) p. 108
26 Hewitt, Peter. *Kenya Cowboy.* (30 Degrees South, Johannesburg, 2008) pp. 109–110
27 Kitson, Major Frank. *Gangs and Counter Gangs.* (Barrie & Rockliff, London, 1960) p. 79
28 Peterbaxterafrica.com
29 Clayton, Anthony. *Counter-Insurgency in Kenya: A Study of Military Operations against Mau Mau 1952–1960.* (Sunflower University Press. Yuma, Manhattan, Kansas, 1984) p. 28
30 Kitson, Major Frank. *Gangs and Counter Gangs.* (Barrie & Rockliff, London, 1960) p. 64
31 Kitson, Major Frank. *Gangs and Counter Gangs.* (Barrie & Rockliff, London, 1960) p. 73
32 Majdalany, Fred. *State of Emergency: The Full Story of the Mau Mau.* (Haughton Mifflin Company, Boston, 1963) p. 219
33 Hewitt, Peter. *Kenya Cowboy.* (30 Degrees South, Johannesburg, 2008) p. 112
34 Hewitt, Peter. *Kenya Cowboy.* (30 Degrees South, Johannesburg, 2008) p. 229
35 Henderson, Ian; Goodhart, Phillip. *Man Hunt in Kenya.* (Bantam Edition, New York, 1988) p. 145
36 Henderson, Ian; Goodhart, Phillip. *Man Hunt in Kenya.* (Bantam Edition, New York, 1988) p. 124
37 Henderson , Ian; Goodhart, Phillip. *Man Hunt in Kenya.* (Bantam Edition, New York, 1988) p. 140
38 Henderson , Ian; Goodhart, Phillip. *Man Hunt in Kenya.* (Bantam Edition, New York, 1988) p. 143
39 Henderson , Ian; Goodhart, Phillip. *Man Hunt in Kenya.* (Bantam Edition, New York, 1988) p. 143
40 Henderson, Ian; Goodhart, Phillip. *Man Hunt in Kenya.* (Bantam Edition, New York, 1988) p. 201
41 Baxter, Peter. *Rhodesia: Last Outpost of the British Empire.* (Galago Press, Johannesburg, 2010) p. 311
42 Anderson, David. *Histories of the Hanged.* (W.W. Norton, New York 2005) p. 295
43 Gunaratna, Rohan; Jerard, Jolene; Rubin, Lawrence. *Terrorist Rehabilitation and Counter-Radicalisation New Approaches to Counter-Terrorism.* (Routledge, London & New York, 2011) p. 4
44 Swynnerton, R.J.M. (1955). The Swynnerton Report: A plan to intensify the development of African agriculture in Kenya. Nairobi: Government Printer.
45 Ogot, B.A. 'The decisive years'. In B.A. Ogot & W.R. Ochieng (Eds.), *Decolonization & Independence in Kenya 1940–93.* (East African Educational Publishers, Nairobi, 1995). pp. 48–79
46 Kenyatta, Jomo, *Suffering Without Bitterness.* (East African Publishing House, Nairobi 1968) p. 189
47 Maloba, Munyabari O. *Mau Mau and Kenya: An Analysis of a Peasant Revolt.* (Indiana University Press, Bloomington, 1998) p. 169

Peter Baxter is an author, amateur historian and African field, mountain and heritage travel guide. Born in Kenya and educated in Zimbabwe, he has lived and travelled over much of southern and central Africa. He has guided in all the major mountain ranges south of the equator, helping develop the concept of sustainable travel, and the touring of battlefield and heritage sites in East Africa. Peter lives in Oregon, USA, working on the marketing of African heritage travel as well as a variety of book projects. His interests include British Imperial history in Africa and the East Africa campaign of the First World War in particular. His first book was *Rhodesia: Last Outpost of the British Empire*; he has written several books in the Africa@War series, including *France in Centrafrique*, *Selous Scouts*, *Mau Mau* and *SAAF's Border War.*